Contents

A Man with
Three Lives

A Man with Three Lives

THE AUTOBIOGRAPHY OF AN OTHERWISE ORDINARY BLOKE

Lindsay Turnbull

To order additional copies of this book, contact:
Xlibris Corporation
1-800-618-969
www.Xlibris.com.au
Orders@Xlibris.com.au
501976

Dedication

*I would like to dedicate this book to my wife, Liz,
and our children Fiona, Bronwyn, Greg and John.*

Acknowledgements

My dear mother, Lexie, my late father, Keith, and my two sisters, Rosalyn and Jill, have been an enormous part of my life and for that, I thank them.

Additionally, I would like to thank my good friend Pat Drew for the *Foreword* to this book.

Last, but not least, I would like to acknowledge my former colleague, Ron Derrick, who gave up his time so generously to review the book.

To all the other people whose names appear in this book, please see it as recognition of the positive influence you have had on my life.

Lindsay Turnbull

Foreword

R-E-S-P-E-C-T. Otis Redding wrote it, Aretha Franklin sang it and Lindsay Turnbull has earned it. From the North Queensland schoolboy to the Mt Isa newcomer to the Sunshine Coast father, sportsman and teacher, Lindsay has gained respect from all he has met. He writes of three lives, yet each of those lives record the same spirit that has persevered in all circumstances.

I first met Lindsay in 1977, but shared a number of common background experiences through family circumstance, sport and profession. North Queensland teachers' sons who played tennis and cricket and attended Townsville University ended up teaching together at Nambour High School and playing for the Nambour Cricket Club, and our friendship has grown through the decades.

Perseverance has been Lindsay's trademark, as an opening batsman, a thinking captain and a patient educator of a sometimes recalcitrant clientele. A dry wit seasoned a sober manner and companions would soon note the twinkle of an intellect that could employ Gilbert and Sullivan with the same verve as Keynesian economic theory, sometimes late at night merging the pair.

Adversity surfaced but was overcome, and life progressed through family and career, always backed by the boundless energy and limitless efforts of his family and friends. To his community was given the expertise that was equally at home coaching sport or handling the finances of clubs or Parents and Citizens' groups. From a Sunshine Coast cricket selector to the Yandina soccer barbeque, a National Titles convenor to the starter at the school sports, the quality of contribution has been the same.

When life took a different branch in 2002, Lindsay faced his greatest challenge as he found his independence threatened, but his network rallied to help prepare the path he must travel alone. On an April Sunday the Nambour Golf Club hosted its biggest ever day as the course was filled morning then afternoon in horrible conditions, by a throng intent on honouring through support a person well respected.

The new life brought its burdens, some known only personally, yet Lindsay has continued to participate in other circles as the layers of life increased. Now he maintains the passage, influencing minds through tutoring, bodies through sports coaching and spirits through example. His story is one of determination, ambition, strength, and, above all, respect.

Pat Drew

A Country Boy

"I'm going to get a belting for this", Lindsay thought as he sped down the road on his sister's bike, carefully avoiding the larger rocks on the road but still pedalling hard despite the downhill run. In his family, the children got a bike when they turned ten and he had a few years to go. For sure, Rosalyn would tell her father when she found out. Lindsay's dad, Keith, had a procedure for issuing beltings. First, he would deliver a verbal tirade, and then confine Lindsay to his room while he seemed to take forever to find a suitable belt. The wait for the inevitable was the worst. After the belting the confinement continued so he, "could reflect on the bad thing he had done", before being released.

At the bottom of the hill was the reward. Feeling carefully under the bridge Lindsay found the packet of cigarettes and the matches. He decided to wait for Brian. Then the major project—catching lobbies in the creek! On the past few occasions, they had seen this huge lobby but had been unable to catch it—maybe today. Lindsay wondered if Brian would bring his air rifle so they could do some shooting.

The six years Lindsay spent at Isis Central Mill, a small town near Childers, whose population consisted of sugar mill workers and sugar cane growers, were the first he could remember of a childhood spent mainly in small country towns. Here he had many experiences. Like the time he set fire to the scrub down by the creek to see what happened! When he arrived home, his family was looking at the neighbours fighting a grassfire which threatened their houses. He tried to look innocent but guessed his mother, Lexie, was, at the very least, suspicious of him. Then there was the time he was sent down to the shop to get the bread and milk. "Mum doesn't need bread or milk today, so she said I could buy some lollies with the money." That bought a lot of lollies! The closer he got to home, the faster the lollies disappeared as Lindsay became increasingly concerned that a huge bag of lollies would be difficult to conceal. And would his mother believe him when he told her he had lost the money on the way to the shop? Little did he know that the shopkeeper had already rung his mother to check out the authenticity of the transaction! Strange that the lady rang after Lindsay had bought the lollies, not before!

Lindsay was born in the Kingaroy Hospital on May 11th, 1951. There were probably many people born on that day—after all, it was the age of the "Baby Boomers". At that time, he had a sister, Rosalyn, three years his elder. Five years later, another sister, Jill, was born. His father, Keith, was a primary school principal, for many years of one-teacher schools. So Lindsay was destined to travel throughout some remote parts of Queensland. His brief stays at Wengenville where his father was teaching when Lindsay was born, and Evergreen were remembered only through the stories told to him by his parents. Keith taught at Rocky Point, Hillsdale, Sarina, Wengenville, Evergreen, Isis Central Mill, Pentland, Bellenden Kerr, Aloomba, Burpengary and Albany Hills.

Lindsay's first memories of Isis Central Mill are of the school where he began his education. His father was his teacher. In 1959 after six years at the school, Lindsay's father was transferred to Pentland. Not long after leaving, the school at Isis Central Mill was closed down. The building was moved to Childers where it was maintained as a museum piece.

How Lindsay remembered the transfer to Pentland! It was like moving to a different world—no electricity, the toilet ("Thunder Box") down in the back yard requiring a night service, and one hundred kilometres from Charters Towers with very little in between. A bore in a dry creek bed supplied the town's water. Sometimes this dried up or the pump would break down. The community was quite poor, with timber-getting, the railway and the Cape River Meatworks, when it was operating, providing most of the jobs. Occasionally movies were shown in the community hall. Unfortunately, a combination of out-dated projection equipment and a projectionist who liked a drink meant there were frequent breakdowns while the tape was repaired. At other times the Country Women's Association organised fancy dress balls or other community activities.

Lindsay's family moved there during the May holidays of 1960. Since their furniture was delayed, they lived in a room at the back of the pub—an experience for a tee-totalling family! Overwhelmed by this transfer, the family forgot Lindsay's 9th birthday. It was celebrated the next day.

When Lindsay arrived in Pentland, Billy and Norman were riding their horses past the pub when they noticed the new boy in town. Since Lindsay seemed intrigued about these two boys riding their horses down the main street like they did in the "Westerns", they offered to race and enquired if he would like to bet on who would win. Clearly, Norman would win because his father was the policeman. This cost Lindsay threepence. However, they were good enough to give him a chance to recoup his loss! Obviously, it was Norman's turn to win. This cost Lindsay another threepence. After it happened again and Lindsay's funds had disappeared into Billy's pocket, the town's new arrival had an unflattering reputation.

God moves in mysterious ways because the next week Lindsay found a ten-shilling note near the back gate of the pub. He took it to the police station sure that someone would be anxious to retrieve it. After a few weeks, the policeman presented the unclaimed money to Lindsay. The next year this money helped him buy his first (and only) bike.

What a passport to freedom this bike proved to be! He and his friends would ride out in the bush for miles—to a lemon tree, to swim in some farmer's irrigation tank or to the new bridge over the Cape River near the meatworks, which had a 100-metre section of sealed road. One of his and his friends' favourite places was the slaughter yards a few kilometres out of town. Here they would try to catch parrots with food placed under a box held up by a stick to which was attached a length of string. It worked only once! Then they had no idea what to do with the bird so it was released.

There were some rough boys who attended the school, none more so than Billy.

During lunch one day at Pentland State School, Keith heard a commotion in the playground and looked out to see Tom, a solid boy with thick glasses, (and thus the victim of much teasing), holding Billy Hughes in an arm lock. This presented a dilemma since Billy was a wild boy who was more likely to be dishing out the violence rather than receiving it. It seemed that Tom just had more than he could tolerate and providence had placed him in this dominant position. As the teacher, Keith knew he had to intercede! But what would Billy do once he was released? Instead of retaliating, Billy stormed off home to get his Dad to, "sort everyone out", as he put it. As it happened Billy's father was at home. He spent long periods in the bush cutting timber. After hearing a distorted version of events, he immediately headed for the school. Lindsay and most of the other twenty-five pupils watched this high drama unfold. Billy's father launched his wrath on Keith while still fifty metres away. Everyone could hear it clearly, alarmed that it contained so much swearing with distinct undertones of menace, and that he seemed intent on following it up with some physical violence. Lindsay's father, a tall well-built athletic man, did not retreat. Instead, he headed towards Billy's father with intent, clearly determined to go on the front foot. It soon turned the confrontation into a discussion. Keith gradually straightened out the story and many other events that had preceded it. As Lindsay's father talked, a rapid transformation in the demeanour of Billy's father occurred. In the end, he took his son home and apparently gave him a good beating. Billy was then taken back out to his father's timber-getters' camp to work for a few weeks. Not something that Keith could condone but it went unreported and its appropriateness couldn't be questioned! Rough justice, but effective!

Billy's time at the loggers' camp must have had a positive impact because he became friendlier with Lindsay after that. One day Lindsay's mother sent him down to Lane's butcher shop to get some provisions for the evening meal. Billy offered him a lift home on the back of his horse. He rode bareback as most boys did, not having enough money to buy a saddle. Billy held the meat while Lindsay scrambled up behind. The horse took exception to this and bucked so that Lindsay was thrown off hitting his head on a rock and splitting it open (his head, not the rock). The Flying Doctor was notified but was unable to come until the next day. They gave instructions to Mrs Mac, an ex-nurse, so she tended to Lindsay overnight.

Anyone who thinks that living in an isolated place without electricity, sealed roads, few sporting facilities and few friends is unattractive evidently hasn't had the privileged life that Lindsay had.

Since Lindsay's father was the principal of small primary schools, he spent his childhood in isolated places. So when holidays (especially Christmas) came around he looked forward to trips to "civilisation". Mostly, the family lived in North Queensland, so the downside of holidays was the long trek down to either the Sunshine or Gold Coasts. The trips were enlivened by games like "white horses" which required passengers to be the first to see a white horse. Often as a result of the competitive nature that his family possessed, a white horse was sighted so far away that it could have been a bullock or a sheep. Sometimes they were lucky enough to be able to listen to a radio broadcast of cricket which was picked up by positioning the transistor radio somewhere on the back hat rack. Lindsay's sisters didn't think this relieved the boredom! They stopped at the usual places each time plus some extras when Jill feigned thirst or the need for a toilet stop. After two days they reached the first of their relatives at Childers, Lindsay's mother's brother and his family. The next day was a leisurely drive to the Leans' farm at Chatsworth where a game of backyard cricket and lunch could be squeezed in before departing for the final destination, 32 Rigby Street, Nambour. This was where Lindsay's maternal grandparents lived.

The weeks at the beach were usually shared with cousins, some of whom liked to play cricket, do jigsaws, play fiddlesticks, or, for all of them, swim and play at the beach. Apart from the occasional picnics, Lindsay was not sure what his parents, uncles and aunts did, but the cousins had no trouble putting in a full day.

Other visits/stays were on the annual agenda. One was to visit the Sullivans at Maidenwell. Trevor and Lindsay would catch old Buddy the poor horse that carried all the children without complaint. When Bill Sullivan told them not to ride Bindy, a young colt, it was like an invitation. So when they got thrown off, they didn't tell anyone. On the horses Lindsay and Trevor were cowboys looking for Indians along the gullies. They never found any!

Eventually all good things come to an end, not only each holiday, but the childhood holidays in general. Would Lindsay like to have this time over again? You bet!!!

Bett's Creek hadn't flowed for many years. However, when one of its downstream tributaries flooded, water started to flow back up the creek. So slowly did it flow that most of the town's population was there to witness the phenomena, many of them standing in the creek bed as the water bubbled along. The arrival of this water provided a range of new activities for Lindsay and his friends—like making billy carts and riding them down the bank to get airborne and land in the water. Then there was fishing with improvised gear like a pin bent over to fashion a hook; or swimming until ear infections became an epidemic.

There was no bridge crossing Bett's Creek on the main road between Charters Towers and Hughenden, so when water covered the crossing, cars became bogged in the creek. A local man set up a business at the crossing. He charged £10 to pull the bogged cars out with his tractor, and £5 to tow them through if they didn't wish to try of their own accord. It was widely suspected that he dug up the crossing during the night to promote business! Lindsay and Kevin hid behind a bush and, sure enough, that's what he did. He saw them and fired a rifle shot over their heads. If this wasn't the time Lindsay's sprinting career started, it certainly contributed to it!

There wasn't much sport played in Pentland. Occasionally, a social cricket match was arranged. In one of these games, Lindsay played his first game of cricket with his father, Keith. Keith was a very good cricketer and must have missed the game terribly during the three years he was stationed there. On another occasion, when Doody's truck was doing the rounds of the town to scrape up a team for another social match, Lindsay climbed on board. His father wasn't too happy about this because he didn't believe sport should be played on a Sunday.

At other times, Doody's truck would do the rounds of the town picking up anyone who wanted to go for a picnic. These were well supported and generally at a swimming hole on the Cape River. Each family brought a hamper which was shared around. Doody's truck also did the *night service* and delivered loads of firewood.

Since there were no high schools in the vicinity, the family had to move back to the coast. Already Lindsay's older sister, Rosalyn, was living with her grandparents and studying for her Junior Examination at Nambour High School.

Keith was temporarily appointed to the one-teacher school at Bellenden Kerr, 10 kilometres north of Babinda, in 1964. What a contrast! At the foothills of the Bellenden Kerr Range, the area was one of the wettest in Australia. It was also one of the prettiest. Most families were wealthy cane farmers.

Lindsay found a different group of friends here. Many of them were of Italian origin, gravitating to the area to work in or own the cane farms. Apart from their heritage, they were no different to any other boys (although some had strange names like the brothers, Funno and Silvo). Swimming in Harvey Creek was fun; jumping into the water from the railway bridge had a sad outcome one day when his pet dog, Lance, wasn't able to get off the bridge as the rail motor came. Lance got most of himself on the edge of a transom but his tail remained on the line and was severed. The dog ran home, and by the time Lindsay got there, it was already on its way to a veterinarian in Innisfail.

Lance was a special dog. He came to the family as a stray. The school was the most likely place for people to dump dogs they couldn't keep since they knew that the students would at least feed them, if not adopt them. Lindsay's father tried hard to keep it out of the school grounds. Eventually, Lindsay and Rosalyn convinced him to keep the dog as their pet. It was not long before the whole family was pleased about that. The dog was a black retriever. It would chase balls or anything thrown until it was exhausted. Lindsay would pretend to throw the ball in one direction and after the dog had run in that direction, throw it elsewhere. He would then watch the dog scout in circles until it found the ball. Sometimes Lindsay would drop the ball in a bucket of water. Lance still retrieved it.

Lance would chase to retrieve anything. One day when the father of one of Aloomba's pupils was mowing the school grounds on their new ride-on mower, he perfected the skill of removing obstacles like sticks from the path the mower would take on its next circuit. As he passed underneath the african tulip tree he picked up and threw away a large stick. Behind him, Lance chased and brought back the stick, placing it in the next path the mower was to take. It took about five or six laps before the man realised what was happening. All the while, Lindsay's father was watching with much amusement.

During cricket practice, Lance would retrieve the ball, depositing it at the feet of the bowler. This saved having a lot of fielders, but the price for that was to bowl a ball the dog had "slobbered over". When it was too tired to continue, Lance would take the ball home and hide it.

The dog possessed a special trick. It could roll over, sit up and beg. Nobody could resist giving it a special treat after that performance. It was allowed inside the house. Each night, when lights were turned out, Lance would go from room to room checking to see if everyone was home. If Rosalyn was still out, he would sit on the front steps until she returned. The dog loved swimming. Sometimes, after school, Lindsay would change into his swimming togs, get a towel from the cupboard in full view of Lance, then hide. The dog would run the three kilometres down to Behana Creek sure that Lindsay must be there already. If he wasn't, the dog would run back home. Some boys can be so cruel! Keith took pity on Lance. He would drive him down to the swimming hole then, afterwards, dry him with a towel so that the dog could ride home in the back of the car.

Eventually the dog got so old it had to be put down. What a sad occasion that was! Lindsay was pleased he had left home before the dog started to lose its sight and hearing.

Many years later, Lindsay's parents drove back up to Aloomba to join in the centenary celebrations for the school. One of the neighbours enquired after Lance's whereabouts. Keith informed him that Lance had died. "In fact", said Keith, "we buried him over there behind that banana tree." The man was aghast! Clearly he had confused the names of Lindsay and Lance.

Bellenden Kerr was a very small school which struggled to remain open. Keith had accepted the transfer even though the school had a lower classification. He still retained his status and level of pay with the promise that, in time, he would be transferred to another larger school in the near vicinity. The Department of Education was true to its word.

Sometimes Lindsay would meet up with some of his mates and ride down to the Bellenden Kerr Landing on the Russell River. Many fishing boats were moored here with dinghies tied to the landing. Lindsay and his friends would climb into a dinghy and row up and down the river. There was never a thought about crocodiles although they knew some people were taken at nearby Deeral Landing on the Mulgrave River. If they did think about the crocodiles there, the fun would have been even greater.

Since there wasn't a Grade Seven class there, Lindsay took the school bus to Babinda (or rode his bike so that he could collect guavas from the side of the road). However, Lindsay's father didn't like their teaching methods so Lindsay completed Grade Seven during the May holidays and joined the Grade 8 class at Bellenden Kerr for the remainder of the year. The education of a pupil in a small school is a rich one offering that provided by larger schools and much more.

One-teacher schools require a lot of preparation by the teacher. All students are in one room, strategically placed so that the teacher could be sure all were on task. Lindsay's father will have filled both blackboards (and perhaps some smaller boards) with the day's work during the previous afternoon. This included work to be done with and without the teacher. All homework was checked before school as the pupils arrived.

When the bell rang in the morning to signify parade, all students lined up in their classes. The two children on roster were ready to raise the Australian flag. The children sang "God Save The Queen" as the flag was raised. Then they recited "The Golden Rule", *"Do unto others as you would have them do unto you"*. Occasionally, there were instructions or severe warnings to be delivered by Keith. He would then disappear into the library to start the record player which crackled out a marching tune, to which all the students marched into the classroom, (school marches were an event at the annual inter-school sports carnival as well as athletics and ball games). Keith would then read a passage from the Bible, explain its significance after which they would recite The Lord's Prayer. Each class had monitors, rotated weekly. These monitors washed and distributed the slates upon which the students wrote. The higher classes had copy books in which they wrote using nibbed pens and ink. The rest of their written work was done in an exercise book writing with a pencil. Hence all desks had inkwells as well as slots for the slates.

The highlight of the day came at the beginning of morning tea. Each student was given, thanks to the Queensland Government, a one-third pint bottle of milk. Not all students liked it, especially if it was a hot day as there was no refrigeration. So some of them had extra bottles! Often Lance, the dog, finished off any remaining milk. Some enterprising students brought flavoured straws which converted the milk into a chocolate or strawberry drink. After school, Lindsay's mother cleaned most of the school while his father cleaned and disinfected the toilets.

The next year, Lindsay attended Babinda School, (with a new high school top), as the first group in Queensland to study Grade 8 at high school. A new building was constructed on the western outskirts of the town, close to the famous Boulders at the base of the Bellenden Kerr Range. This site eventually became Babinda High School.

After only one year at Bellenden Kerr, Keith was transferred to Aloomba, a few kilometres north. This was another spectacular location with Walsh's Pyramid looming above the school. After rain, the water cascaded down the rocky face. Climbing the pyramid was exciting and not too strenuous in the beginning. However, as friends and relatives visited, the obligatory climb lost its appeal. Lindsay attended Gordonvale State School to complete Year 8 as the newly-built high school couldn't yet accommodate them. In 1965, the class moved to the High School where he completed his high school education.

Two teachers there had a great influence on Lindsay's future. One was the Principal, Jim Bourner, who was also his Senior Maths teacher. Such was his passion for mathematics that Lindsay followed a similar path in his career as a Maths teacher. Jim Bourner was so proud of his first school as principal that he volunteered the students, (and some of their parents), to lay a cricket pitch, turf the ovals, and build the tennis and basketball courts.

He bestowed the critical job of ringing the school bell on Lindsay. Perhaps it was because Lindsay had a watch, (a prize from a successful response to a Milo competition). What a joy it was to terminate a lengthy lesson by ringing the bell, (except when Bill Webb had removed the gong)!

One day when most of the school's male population was playing a form of American Basketball, the Principal leaned out his window and shouted to Lindsay, "When are we going to have a bell?" Before discretion tempered his response, Lindsay replied, "There is one minute to go!" What a mistake! He was called to the Principal's office. As befitted his manner as a principal, Mr Bourner simply rang the dedicated number that gave the exact Eastern Standard Time. Needless to say, he was right!

The other teacher was a short, powerfully built man who taught a wide variety of subjects. It was rumoured that he possessed, at some time, a boxing title of some significance. Kevin Murgatroyd did nothing to confirm or deny the rumour. On reflection, Lindsay thought that he probably used it to his advantage. He never seemed to get angry but retained complete discipline. As he walked past, all the boys could be seen pulling up their socks and tucking in their shirts. He achieved good results for most of his students. His demeanour took on a more humane face when he, Jim Bourner and other teachers involved Lindsay and many of the senior students in bushwalking, including a climb to the top of Mt Bartle Frere (the highest mountain in Queensland).

Sport was a significant part of Lindsay's life (and all his family as well)—at school and on weekends. He played most sports at school with some success in athletics. When told there would be some interschool cricket involving Cairns State High, Trinity Bay State High and his school, Lindsay immediately appointed himself captain and began organizing a team. When he passed on the details of the team to Mr Bourner, the principal politely enquired as to who made him the captain and sole selector. Lindsay didn't know what to say because he thought it was obvious and at no stage had he thought he was big-noting himself.

On Saturday, Lindsay played cricket and tennis. The whole family played tennis. Lindsay had the pleasure of whitening everyone's tennis shoes on Saturday morning. The family played for Excelsiors Tennis Club in Gordonvale. The local doctor, Ray (Doc) Davis, his wife Gill and many of their family also played in the same team. Lindsay played a lot with Doc enjoying some success. However, the day they beat the Langtrees, Doc perambulated about the tennis courts describing to anyone who cared to listen, how tactics always triumphed over stroke-making ability (which Lindsay considered underestimated his talents in the stroke-making area).

The Davis's were a wonderful family. Doc and Gill emigrated from England mainly because of Doc's ailing health. He had endured a serious operation on his lungs. As a result, his ability to play tennis at all was noteworthy, let alone being able to play A-Grade. On the other hand, Gill was a natural sportswoman, having the rare distinction of scoring a century at Lords. She was a talented tennis player also, enjoying much success both in Gordonvale and Cairns. All five children played sport, generally with much success. They were academically gifted as well. Yvonne was in the same year level as Lindsay. She also attended James Cook University, boarded at John Flynn College, transferred to Queensland University to complete a Diploma in Education and became a teacher. She moved quickly through the ranks to eventually become Deputy Principal. Doc was also Lindsay's family doctor. His favourite prescription was to *play more sport!* So dedicated was he to his profession, that he refused to retire until a serious accident made it impossible for him to continue. When Lindsay's parents were on holidays, he was often given invitations for meals and social activities at the Davis's.

When he turned 13, Lindsay's father allowed him to play in the local cricket team. Lindsay's first ball faced in senior cricket was against a retired Sheffield Shield captain, Jim Bratchford. Then, at the other end, was an aspiring Sheffield Shield bowler, Phil Minnecon. It was a very successful start to Lindsay's career since he walked off the field with his health intact. Although he became only a very average cricketer, the sport became his preferred option and he played every year until he was fifty (years old).

Sport at school for half the school year was swimming—at the Greenpatch in the Mulgrave River. The students all went down at the start of lunch for some rides on the big rope which dropped them in the middle of the river. The fun stopped when Mr Murgatroyd arrived. "Up to the water pipe and back"! Lindsay wasn't a strong swimmer so that even when the river wasn't fresh from above-average rainfall, it was a difficult task.

The Greenpatch was also the regular meeting place for the Year 12's after school on Fridays where they had mud fights. This was suspended for some time when a passing car was hit. After the driver reported it to the police, some of them were spoken to and warned. At other times, they gathered at the Pyramid Café which had just installed a pinball machine. Bill Webb was the champion and could build up his free games to as many as 10. Failing that, if the rest of us coughed and generally made a loud noise, Bill knew where to give the machine a solid blow so that it offered up a free game. In years to come, Bill expanded on this discovery to locate public telephones that would allow free calls.

High school at Gordonvale was a memorable experience for Lindsay. He was an above-average student whose greatest strength was in mathematics. It should have been in the sciences as well but circumstances, including a limited choice of subjects, (since Gordonvale High School was so small), a desire to continue with Geography, and a Junior science teacher whose principle learning support equipment was a metre-long three by one inch piece of timber resulted in that not occurring.

When his high school education finished after the public exams of 1968, the Year 12's went on their separate ways. Lindsay and a handful of others were accepted into the University of Queensland at Townsville (later to become The James Cook University). Boarding the train for Townsville with Yvonne Davis and Bill filled Lindsay with excitement and anticipation of a new phase of his life.

John Flynn College, quite a new residential college, had rooms, facilities and a general ambience that could easily distract a student, not only a "fresher", from the intended purpose of being at university. Lindsay didn't come from an impoverished household, but ceiling fans and special study suites in his room were bordering on luxury.

Lindsay couldn't wait to put his possessions in his room and embark on an expedition to meet other new arrivals and discover all the facilities. A partitioned common room contained a television room, (Lindsay didn't have a TV set at home), and a table tennis court. Outside were a soft drink machine and a public telephone. Next door was a large, well-furnished dining room, which, he was sure, would offer meals to match. Of less interest were the laundry facilities at the back (which Lindsay would later embellish). This was also a co-educational college which would increasingly offer a different lifestyle.

When he returned to his room, Lindsay was horrified to find all his clothes, books and personal belongings strewn all around the room. He was getting his first taste of Orientation week, a time when freshers were subjected to experiences that other university people believed would start new students on an appropriate footing. While staring at this mess, Lindsay turned the fan on. Washing powder was spread all over the room! One reaction would have been to get angry, wanting to find the culprits! Fortunately, Lindsay did not choose this option but proceeded to clean everything up (not before many other students witnessed the aftermath of the prank). He even suffered the wrath of the cleaner who vacuumed up the washing powder the next morning. In this way Lindsay passed the first test. Later he discovered that was what older students felt obliged to do to first-years. In later years, Lindsay had the opportunity to pass on the tradition.

University was a wonderful way to spend four years, especially if it was experienced from the inside of a residential college. Lindsay found himself caught between the attractions that were on offer and the education it was meant to provide, no doubt a dilemma that confronted most students, especially freshers. Just the interaction among students of a similar impressionable, experimental and reactionary age was exciting.

On top of this were the distractions of all the sporting and social activities, the college activities like "At Homes", and university student groups of various interests.

The Student Council of James Cook University organised a number of events throughout the year such as Orientation Week and Commemoration Week. They also staged an event called, "The Boat Races". Not many people knew how it got that name since it had nothing to do with boats or even water. It was a series of competitions about who could drink the most beer and who could drink it fastest alone or in a group. The contests were mostly between the residential colleges. The main race involved drinking from the yard glass. This vessel held a large amount of beer mostly in a rounded bottom above which was a long, narrow neck. There was clearly an art to performing it successfully. The fact that you liked beer was insufficient.

John Flynn College was well represented by a final year student who seemed to be able to drink without swallowing, if such a thing is possible! He was best with the yard glass, and helped the College to win the pairs, fours and eights. Lindsay was a successful member of the winning eights, although by no means a fast drinker. On reflection, it seemed a terrible waste of beer.

Lindsay was a keen and capable sportsman, an ability inherited from and fostered in his family. His father was quite a good cricketer, an accomplished tennis player, a professional athlete and had a highly competitive spirit that enabled him to turn his hand comfortably to most sports (except golf, no matter how much he tried). Lindsay's mother was a very good tennis player who, according to a Cairns' professional, could have played at a high level. She also became a very handy player at vigoro, a popular female version of cricket in the Cairns' area. Both Lindsay's sisters played tennis and vigoro quite well, with Jill going on to become a very good tennis player especially at the veterans' level. So it wasn't surprising that Lindsay played all the sport he could, unafraid to try new sports like squash or volleyball. In his third year he became the president of the Sports' Committee at James Cook University.

The university was very new and located far enough out of town to become its own entity. Only a couple of students owned cars and they generally asked for petrol money. So water fights were often the Friday, Saturday and Sunday night entertainment.

Water fights were not condoned by the College hierarchy. So things like escape routes were important to learn. Lindsay's room on C Deck was directly above the pathway which led from the male quarters to the Common Room. However, since it was on the third story, it was difficult to douse someone with a bucket of water as he emerged from underneath. If the stair lights were on, that unsuspecting person's shadow would indicate their impending emergence in time to release the contents of the bucket. On one particular Friday night, Lindsay sensed someone outside his room so he locked the door. The exclamations of surprise/dismay by the victim downstairs and the sound of running feet which obviously belonged to the bomber, prompted Lindsay to venture outside to see what had happened. Up the stairs strode a very wet senior resident tutor with water still dripping from his beard. In his mind Lindsay was obviously the perpetrator. Meanwhile the real one was at that moment climbing down the laundry chute.

So Lindsay appeared before the Principal the next day. His guilt wasn't discussed, just his punishment. The Principal decided that Lindsay should participate in landscaping outside the laundry at the back of A Deck. There he built a rock garden! Is it still there today? Probably not, since he had neither the skill nor the heart to complete the project to the point where one might be inclined to pay the landscaper!

Lindsay's trips to town were generally for cricket, (playing for Brothers with a university friend, Col Lyons) or tennis, (playing for University in the Townsville competition). Col was best man at Lindsay and Liz's wedding. Later, in his third year, he and many other students would go into town to watch the University Rugby League play successfully in the Townsville competition, or to go to the Vale, the uni students' local pub.

Lindsay studied Economics. He had accepted a Teachers' Fellowship which required him to complete a degree, a Diploma in Education and then teach for the Department of Education for at least four years. As a result, he was paid an allowance of $19.50 per week as well as having his university fees paid. In his first year of university, Lindsay had to study three teaching subjects. He chose economics, maths and geography. In the end, he remained a teacher throughout his working life, mainly teaching Maths and Economics.

Christmas holidays for university students were very long and generally designed to allow students to get a job to help pay for university expenses. After his first year, Lindsay got a job in Cairns as a storeman for a dodgy firm. Since he had a driver's licence, he was expected to do deliveries in a truck. His off-sider, David, was a young lad from Thursday Island, brought down by a host family to gain work experience. One day the two left the storehouse with a load of prams at peak traffic time. Each thought the other had tied down the load. At the first intersection, braking caused all the prams to scatter in parts across the intersection. After a few seconds it seemed useless to look at each other, especially since the boss was in his car behind us. So we began to retrieve the parts. If we had any downtime during the next week, we were expected to try to put the prams back together again. On another occasion, although it was knock-off time, Lindsay and his co-worker were asked to deliver some mattresses to a new set of flats. First they had to visit another storehouse to pick up the mattresses. It seemed odd that they had to cut off the labels first. The driveway to the newly-built flats wasn't completed, so as Lindsay reversed, David directed. After a short time he motioned to stop. Coming around to the driver's window, he said, "You just knocked down the fence"! We unloaded the mattresses and left as quickly as possible.

After his second year, Lindsay got a job on the railway, the Number 7 Bridge Gang. On the first day, the Ganger had to sign him on. The foreman's eyesight was so bad that very thick glasses weren't good enough to read the forms, so he used a magnifying glass. Then they headed off for some maintenance work, hammering down the dogspikes on a bridge at Edmonton. The other eight men who made up the bridge gang wasted little time before testing Lindsay out! A spiking hammer has a weight considerably less than a sledgehammer with a small head so as to be able to hit the dogspikes tucked under the rail of the railway line. When he swung from a small height or missed the spikes or clipped the side of the railway line, Lindsay provided great entertainment. He soon learnt that what looked like an easy job certainly wasn't. The gang was responsible for maintaining rail bridges in the far north of Queensland. At times it was so hot that the railway lines would melt their sandshoes. Lindsay soon learnt to stand the crowbar up when it wasn't being used. The redeeming feature was that there was frequently a creek to swim in.

The Ganger was responsible for getting the train times before we left the Station each morning. At one time they were doing some maintenance on the bridge over Babinda Creek. His difficulty in reading meant that we had removed one transom from the middle of the bridge when a train appeared around the corner. Lindsay and others in the gang threw all the tools and themselves into the creek. If the passengers could have seen how the tracks bent as the train passed over the section that was being repaired, they would have expected to join us. The reward was to spend an inordinate amount of time swimming around retrieving the tools. At another job, they were working on the North Johnson River Bridge. As they removed the old dogspikes to replace the transoms, they threw them in the river. Later the Ganger discovered there weren't sufficient new spikes so they had to jump in the river to find the old dogspikes. The river was home to crocodiles which we later discovered to be harmless. At the time however, it seemed a good reason for danger money.

After smoko at 2.00 pm, it was time to pack up the trolley and head back to the station. The gang lived in railway carriages on the station siding, dirty and cockroach-ridden. There, the nipper would start a fire to boil up water for their showers. The Ganger was allowed to have his shower before 4.00 pm, knock-off time. Then he headed off to the pub while the rest waited for their turn which occurred in order of seniority. By the time it was Lindsay's turn, the nipper had also gone to the pub. He was never seen to have a shower. Perhaps he thought the occasional swims were sufficient. So Lindsay boiled water for himself, cooled it by adding tank water, and filled up the bucket in the corrugated iron cubicle under the tank. The water didn't last long so he had to be quick with the soap. After that, he could join the others at the pub for a few drinks, a meal and entertainment of sorts, usually playing eight-ball. George was a pro, both at eight-ball and at work. At work, he took charge of the chainsaw, a new acquisition for the gang. At the start of work each day, George had to sharpen and clean the chainsaw. This took some time but only because it was such a vital job. When the Ganger said it was time to get back to work, George was just starting to roll a smoke. By the time he got back on top of the bridge all the jobs were started. Lindsay once had the pleasure of playing eight-ball with George against a couple of locals for a stake of £5 each. Lindsay broke, one of their opponents had his turn, and then George sank all eight balls winning a healthy bet for Lindsay and him.

During one holiday break, Lindsay joined two of his friends, Fergus Burgher and Bill Schwenke on a boat trip around the Whitsundays. Fergus' father had a boat which they launched at Shute Harbour. They passed Daydream Island and set up camp on North Molle Island. The island was inhabited only by goats. Their crude attempts at fishing around the island provided very little, so the next day they moved camp to Middle Molle Island. A popular tourist resort was located close by on South Molle Island. They could motor across, swim in the pool and generally pass themselves off as tourists (without the largesse). One day, they went back to Airlie Beach, anchored the boat off the beach, and drove the truck into Proserpine. A teacher they knew was living and teaching in Proserpine. So they visited her and, with her flatmates, went out for the night. The invitation to stay overnight was accepted. Unbeknown to them, a cyclone moved through the Whitsundays that night. When they arrived back at Airlie Beach, the boat was pulled well up the beach. Apparently Fergus' father was contacted by the Air/Sea Search and Rescue the previous night and had spent quite some time holding the boat before he got help to tow the boat up the beach. Not knowing this, the three boys used the truck to push the boat back into the water and set off through the heavy seas to retrieve their belongings, or what remained of them, from the island. When they arrived back at Shute Harbour, they were met by a very irate group from the Air/Sea Search and Rescue who had been searching for them after discovering that the boat had been re-launched from Airlie Beach.

Lindsay finished his Economics Degree at the end of 1971 and moved to Brisbane to do his teacher training. Moving from James Cook University to the University of Queensland in 1972 was like the transition from primary to secondary schooling for Lindsay. He took up residence at Kings College after a taxi ride from Nambour. All trains and buses weren't running because of flooding in the south-east of Queensland. Two other students from Townsville also moved into Kings to complete their Diplomas of Education. This one-year post-graduate diploma course was designed for teachers who had done no formal teacher training throughout their degree.

Third-year students at Kings, including John Buchanan who went on to achieve great success as a cricket coach, thought that Lindsay and his compatriots from Townsville should be treated as "freshers" and complete all the initiation ceremonies that first-year students were forced to endure. They got no response.

Kings, unlike John Flynn, was an all-male residential college. This enhanced its appeal to Lindsay but strangely, provided more distractions. In fact, the best way to study was to go to the university library. The billiard table was very popular. The tennis court had been resurrected with weeds removed, the fence repaired and new net posts and net to complete the job. Lindsay used it often, tennis being one of his favourite sports. It was never difficult to find an opponent, from either the College or the University.

Lindsay had a first floor room with a spectacular view over the Brisbane River. Coal barges were frequently seen, loaded almost to the waterline, on their way downstream from the mines at Ipswich. Occasionally, rowing squads, urged on by someone in a power boat, made their way up or down stream, although this often happened before Lindsay arose.

During his studies, Lindsay was required to do some practice teaching at Brisbane State High School as a part of the course. This was a very large high school, one of the GPS (Greater Public Schools), so that quite a few graduate students were appointed there. They were allocated a room on the top floor of one of the new buildings thus being quite isolated from most of the school. This was not what practice teaching was supposed to be about. In the Year 8 section of the school, located on the other side of the road, a sergeant-major type teacher exercised strict control over both students and practice teachers, or so it seemed. The Maths teacher/mentor seemed to take advantage of Lindsay's presence and he was left to take the class by himself. He later found out that one of the students, Mark Zillman, was a second cousin.

The Diploma in Education course was completed and Lindsay was required to choose the region where he would start his teaching career in 1973. Students were advised not to choose Brisbane, the Sunshine or Gold Coasts since there was an overwhelming demand by existing teachers for those locations. So Lindsay had the bright idea to list those as his first three preferences and then start on the areas that he really wanted to go to—Mackay, Townsville or Cairns. He was posted to Wynnum High School in Brisbane. Peter Rose with whom he had completed an Economics Degree in Townsville and the Diploma in Education course at Brisbane was to start his teaching career at nearby Cleveland High School.

At the end of his last year at the University of Queensland, Lindsay arrived home at Aloomba to find that weather had disrupted the cane-harvesting season to such an extent that farmers were desperate to get off as much cane as possible before the mill closed before Christmas. It was possible to leave some cane, called standover cane, for the following season, but it was preferable to harvest it and replant another crop. So Lindsay got a job hauling-out bins. This involved taking a bin full of harvested cane on a trailer, carting it to a tramline siding, pushing the bin off the trailer and onto the tram line, and then replacing it with an empty bin. At the end of the day, a tram would pick up the full bins and take them to the mill. Sounds simple? The number of times the full bins came off the rails, some even tipping over, made his weekly pay quite generous. The farmer never seemed to get upset when he had to arrive in his tractor to help repair the damage. Not so the harvester driver, Ralph, who gave Lindsay a demonstration of how fast the tractor could go, even towing a full bin along the headland, the narrow track on the verge above the creek bank. He must have been mad!! It was hard and very hot work but Lindsay appreciated the money.

Before he moved south to teach in Brisbane, Lindsay's father paid the deposit on a car. It was a good second-hand car and, of course, it was a Holden (the only type that his father bought). Lindsay paid the instalments on the loan and then the deposit back to his father over the next two years.

Accommodation in Brisbane was very difficult to find so Lindsay and Peter lived in a caravan in someone's backyard for two months. Each morning they awoke early, bought a newspaper and made many unsuccessful telephone calls. In a sellers' market, not many landlords wanted to offer a rental property to two young men. Eventually they found a house to rent in Coorparoo. Another teacher from Wynnum High School soon moved in to occupy the third room. This house was ideal. It looked over Brisbane and was close to the Gabba for cricket and the greyhounds, newly located at the same venue. As well, they were close to Langlands Park, the home ground for Easts Rugby League Club which Lindsay supported.

Lindsay went to teach at Wynnum High School quite underprepared. His practice teaching was grossly insufficient, the academic aspects of the Diploma in Education course was of little assistance, very little help was provided by either the administration or the senior staff, and he was, by nature, over-confident. The net result was an unpleasant first year of teaching. He was allocated mainly Year 8 classes to whom he taught Maths and Geography. He also had a Year 11 Economics class, his preference since they were so well behaved and Lindsay was well qualified in that field. It was a relief when, at the end of the school year, the principal informed him of a transfer, albeit to Mt Isa State High School.

He spent the latter part of the Christmas holidays in Canberra as his sister, Rosalyn, was having her first baby, Tony. As he drove back up north, he became increasingly aware of the storm that was brewing in

Queensland. Stopping to pick up his belongings in Brisbane, he heard
news of a cyclone moving down the Queensland coast. The further
north he drove, the heavier the rain became and, worryingly, the more
swollen the creeks and rivers were. Lindsay reached Bowen and stayed
overnight with his good friend from university days, Fergus. The next
day, the Bruce Highway was cut by the Don River just north of Bowen.
After contacting the Regional Education Office in Townsville, Lindsay
left his car at Bowen and boarded a plane for Townsville.

Flights to Mt Isa were postponed because of flooding at the Mt Isa
airport, a rare occurrence for the town in the hot and dry north-west of
Queensland. At Townsville Lindsay met two of his university friends who
were also posted to teach at Mt Isa, Allan Vitale and Jeff Coward. He
was also interviewed by an Education Department inspector, not only
about the completion of his transfer, but also about his future after Mt
Isa. The town was considered isolated to the point where, after one year,
a teacher could apply, and would be given a transfer out to a region
closer to the coast. After two years, teachers would be given a transfer to
a region of their choice.

Lindsay was booked onto an additional flight which happened to
be the first into Mt Isa. It was greeted by a large number of the local
population who seemed to be using the airport bar as a "local". The next
day, Lindsay visited his new principal, Jim Bourner, who had been his
Maths teacher and principal at Gordonvale.

Accommodation in the form of houses and duplexes were provided
for teachers in Mt Isa. Lindsay was to share a house with two teachers,
one an elderly Dutchman waiting for his family to arrive from Nambour,
and the other a first-year primary school teacher. When he visited his
two friends, however, he discovered that they were sharing a new house
with a yet-to-arrive teacher transferred in from the surrounding area. So
Lindsay moved in. Nobody seemed concerned and the displaced teacher
found a vacant room in another new house across the street.

The extent of the rain and subsequent flooding caused the
Government to cancel the first week of school. Mt Isa was isolated by
road and rail. The mining company dispatched workers to help restore
the railway line and the roads. It also chartered a large cargo plane to
bring in the town's supplies. All residents were notified when fresh milk
or fruit and vegetables arrived in town. Eventually cars started to arrive
by train, including Lindsay's.

Mt Isa was unlike many other towns. It was quite large with a
population of over twenty thousand. The Leichhardt River flowed
through the town, dividing it into "mineside", where the wealthier mine
workers lived, and "townside", where the public servants mostly lived.

The cost of living was very high, geared to the relative wealth of the miners. There were several opulent hotels, each of which became the local to various groups of people. There were also many clubs, mostly ethnic, reflecting the diversity of people employed by Mt Isa Mines. Generally speaking, all students were guaranteed a job in the mines. The nature of that job, however, did depend partly on their educational achievements. It would be true to say there wasn't a predominant desire for good results by students. Still the whole ambience of the school did not cause teachers much stress or frustration. Its location, however, did! The mine's output was mainly copper. It was smelted in Mt Isa so as to reduce the haulage cost to Townsville. The smelter gave off choking sulphur fumes. Depending on the weather, it was prone to settle on the school nearby. A detector located near the school was supposed to alert mining authorities to shut down the smelter. This didn't always happen. So this problem combined with the extreme heat, convinced the Department of Education to air-condition the school. Water-cooled air conditioners were placed in most rooms so that they could be closed off to avoid the fumes. Nevertheless, temperatures still exceeded 38°C in the classrooms during the peak of summer. Those who taught outside, such as the physical education teachers, had no such protection.

Mt Isa had many sporting facilities. Most of these were built and/ or maintained by Mt Isa Mines. Lindsay took advantage of this, playing cricket, tennis, squash and a new game called touch football. It was during this time that he enjoyed some memorable occasions in his cricket career.

The local radio station, 4LM, was owned by a Brisbane radio station, 4IP. When Kerry Packer's organisation started World Series Cricket, Jeff Thompson, Australia's highly successful opening bowler, was signed up by 4IP to keep him playing for Queensland and Australia. He and Dennis Lillee had returned from an "Ashes" series in England where they had played a major role in the defeat of Australia's traditional enemy. As a promotional gesture, he and another imported Queensland player, Vivian (now Sir Vivian) Richards, a prominent batsman in the West Indies team, were sent to Mt Isa. A cricket match was organised with Jeff Thompson the star attraction. Two teams were selected from the local competition and Thommo was to bat and bowl in both teams. It was a nerve-tingling experience for Lindsay, an opening batsman, to face the world's fastest bowler. With the wicketkeeper and slips fieldsmen in the distance and Thommo bowling with that action that caused batsmen to see the ball coming out of his hand very late, success was not getting hit. Lindsay did slightly better than this. He preserved his wicket as well.

Later in the year some State players including Phil Carlson visited and displayed their superior skills. Facing Phil, (a medium-paced bowler according to the commentators), Lindsay had his wickets shattered first ball, which, by his standards was quite fast.

Most teachers in both the secondary and primary schools were quite young, being in their first or second years of teaching. The Department of Education provided accommodation in the form of basic three-bedroom houses or duplexes. This combination led to abundant socialising, even during the week. Next door to Lindsay in Darling Crescent was a house occupied by three young female teachers. One, a Physical Education teacher at the high school was Elizabeth Sinclair. After a short time she and Lindsay became very good friends. This friendship soon grew into a romance, an engagement and a marriage on January 4th, 1975. Liz's parents lived in Inverell, New South Wales. Her father was a doctor there and quite a severe man. If he wanted his scotch whisky with two cubes of ice, Lindsay was expected to know the correct size of ice cubes to use. After a thorough examination, Lindsay was still not sure whether he had made the grade, but, since he wasn't asked to leave pressed on with his proposal for marriage.

The wedding was held in Inverell and Lindsay was pleased that many of his friends from Queensland were able to travel down. The Church of England minister was a Sinclair family friend who had become a Bishop in Adelaide. Unfortunately, this meant there were no rehearsals prior to the wedding day. Even more unfortunate was the fact that his plane was forced to land in Glenn Innes, so that someone had to drive over to collect him. The wedding was delayed a few hours. This wasn't so bad since Lindsay had more time to watch the Test Match between Australia and England, remembered for the heroics of the local boy, Rick McCosker, returning to bat after fracturing his jaw earlier in the match.

Lindsay and Liz enjoyed a honeymoon at the Orchid Beach Resort on Fraser Island. What a spectacular place! No wonder the island is now heritage-listed! The married couple then returned to Mt Isa to look for married accommodation. After a few moves, since such accommodation was difficult to find, they were offered the use of a State Government house which was intended to be used by a mining inspector. He and his family had preferred to rent an air-conditioned up-market house.

Liz was also an avid sports-lover and very good at a range of sports, especially softball in which she was chosen to compete in the Queensland Championships. She and Lindsay also played tennis.

A number of teachers spent their Saturday afternoons at the races. Not all were avid punters but it was a place where you were most likely to find drinking companions. After one of these days, someone suggested that they pool together and buy a racehorse. A meeting was organized to make the necessary arrangements. It was soon obvious that no one had any experience. Someone knew a veterinarian in Brisbane. Another person knew a local trainer. They decided to purchase the horse from Brisbane on the advice of the vet. A short time later the vet reported that there was to be a clearance sale in Brisbane. He was commissioned to check the offerings and make a recommendation on the basis that we were prepared to spend no more than $1600. He supplied them with two possibilities. One was well bred while the other had an unknown pedigree. Lindsay suggested that if the well-bred horse was any good, it would be more expensive. To a group of intelligent teachers, this seemed a logical theory so they proceeded with the purchase of a horse by Burgess Point out of Gayness. The horse was called Gay Point, a name which later needed constant explanation.

The horse was floated to Townsville, and then transferred to a train bound for Mt Isa. The trainer was Ross Kyle, a worker in the mines and a trainer of about five horses in his spare time. He unloaded the horse from the train at Cloncurry since the railway line detoured to Duchess rather than going directly to Mt Isa. The first sight of their 'shortcut to wealth and stardom' was that of a mal-nourished, long-haired and tired-looking nag!

As the days passed a transformation of the horse occurred. Hopes rose as Gay Point ate well, developed a shiny coat and looked forward to daily runs around the track onto which backed Ross' home and stables. At this stage a strange thing happened. The person who was "managing" the syndicate wanted to pull out. Lindsay bought his share and became the "manager". For Lindsay, this meant more visits to the stable. He would take a carrot from his garden each time as a treat for the horse. He was also the only person with whom the trainer would discuss plans. Ross did this by sending his wife over to say, "Ross wants to see you". One of these occasions was memorable when Ross said, "I'll never ride this horse, (he called him Bobby—the nickname given to Phar Lap), again. This morning I let him go at the top of the straight and when I looked down at the ground, I couldn't believe how fast we were going. We have potentially the best horse I have ever seen". Presumably this meant the best in Mt Isa which may have won them some $1000 races. Mt Isa was a wealthy city; no unemployment, well-paid mine workers, successful business people feeding off the wealth created by the mines and with civil servants making up the remaining population. Races were conducted at the Mt Isa Racetrack every Saturday with reasonable attendances and huge turnovers with the bookmakers. As a result, prize money was very good considering the small fields.

As the time for Gay Point's first race, (he was still an unraced four-year-old maiden), approached, the connections started to plan the "big plunge". How naive they were to think that nobody had seen or heard about the horse! What if Ross was planning a betting coup of his own? The jockey, "Stumpy" Bachelor, they later discovered bet heavily although rules outlawed it. The Club's program showed that there would not be a Maiden race over a sprint distance for some weeks. They weren't prepared to wait, so Gay Point was nominated in an 8th

Division, (for horses who had won no more than one race or which hadn't won for quite some time), over 900m. The field was surprisingly large. Gay Point drew barrier 8. They hadn't given it a barrier trial or even a jump-out of the barriers, but Ross was confident it had the right temperament.

In the betting ring that day, eight hopeful debutantes (as owners), with pockets full of money, waited for the bookmakers to offer lucrative odds against the horse winning. **It opened up as a short-priced favourite!** Still, they bet.

What a race!! Beyond their wildest dreams, they watched as their horse jumped in front. The further the race extended, the larger was the gap between Gay Point and the rest of the field. As the horse raced down the straight, the commentator was heard to say, "I don't know where this horse has come from, but it is about to break the Australasian record!" Gay Point won by about ten lengths. The celebrations exceeded the winnings that day but the excitement knew no bounds.

Two more starts at Mt Isa for wins by many lengths (and a starting price of 20/1 on), and it was time to try something more financially rewarding. In a "sting" that gave them great satisfaction and some tidy winnings, they nominated the horse to race the next week at Mt Isa, Cairns, Townsville and Rockhampton. The next night, the horse was floated out of Mt Isa by Ross bound for Rockhampton. When Ross arrived, he settled the horse in a friend's stable (without telling him the horse's real name—don't trust anyone in the racing game). Gay Point had an easy workout around the track, being very fit and having such a good temperament as to make a fast workout unnecessary.

On Thursday afternoon, Jeff and Lindsay drove out of Mt Isa arriving late in Townsville. Here they stayed overnight, picked up Allan, (who had resigned from teaching and was now working on his father's cane farm at Ingham), and headed for Rockhampton the next day. A friend from university days put them up, but not before he had organised a few friends of his to attend the race meeting the next day. Six of them turned up quite early for the races. "Bobby" was in the first race. The race book outlined the horse's form that obviously described that of another far less capable one. Lindsay surveyed the local betting ring, making a note of all the bookmakers and their locations. Back in the bar, each was given his cash and betting instructions. Nobody was in the local betting ring so they stood in the interstate ring behind the fluctuations board. As the horses trotted around to the starting barriers, it was time to bet. Odds varied from 9/4 to 7/4. When Lindsay gave the signal, all six moved to their assigned bookies and bet. Some bet with two bookmakers, but the bagmen were taken completely by surprise so that none could lay off their bets. The boys moved to the fence just in time to see the horses jump. Gay Point was first out and gradually increased his lead to win by twelve lengths. Lindsay collected all the betting tickets—quite a fistful! When "correct weight" was declared, they proceeded to collect—Lindsay with the tickets, big Al Vitale collecting the money and Jeff recording the amounts. They met Ross at the stables, delivering him generous congratulations and his share of the money, *and headed for the car park. They set out immediately for home. Lindsay had a great pile of cash in his lap and the three were in great spirits. The "sting" was complete.*

After another start at Rockhampton for another win at unbackable odds, Gay Point was floated to Brisbane. Racing at Albion Park on a sand surface was generally a mid-week event. However, once each year, a Saturday meeting featuring the Albion Park Cup was held there. The syndicate had timed it nicely. The horse was nominated in a Novice Handicap over the 1460m distance. A large crowd was in attendance that day including Lindsay and Jeff who had flown down from Mt Isa. A massive amount of money, (at least that is what the bookmakers told Lindsay), was wagered on Gay Point at about 7/4. Only a small portion of this came from the connections of the horse. Most originated from bookmakers in Mt Isa and Rockhampton. The odds were quite reasonable, despite the quality of the field, since the horse had won each of his five starts by a total of more than fifty lengths. This day was to be no exception. Gay Point jumped clearly in front of the field and increased his lead to win by nine lengths. The time he ran would have won the main sprint event quite comfortably. How they celebrated! They flew home to a hero's welcome since the horse was considered to have represented Mt Isa in the "big smoke". Alas this was the pinnacle of the horse's career. He did win more races, but he couldn't handle hard or even grass tracks. On the sand tracks he raced with big weights. He won his last race over a longer distance at Albion Park. His final years were spent as a stockhorse at Mackay.

So why didn't we finish up wealthy? Well the Sport of Kings requires the assets of a king to keep a racehorse on the track. Lindsay never considered buying an interest in another horse—it could never have been that much fun again.

To suggest that Mt Isa was a frontier town would neglect to mention some attractive features. It was not uncommon for a group of teachers to go for BBQ's and swims after school at Lake Moondara or the "Calcite Pit". The long afternoons allowed for such activities as a game of cricket or softball. On weekends, trips to the Gregory River or Lawn Hill were possible, provided they didn't interfere with sport. During the Easter holidays of 1974, Lindsay and Liz with another couple drove to Alice Springs. There they chartered a plane to fly up the Todd River Gorges, then to the Olgas, (now called Katatjuta), and Ayers Rock (Uluru) where they were unable to land on the flooded airstrip, and back to Alice Springs. Deserts offer fascinating landscapes. The dry but distinct water courses, the profiles of the sand dunes and the variety of colours can be an interesting contrast to vegetated country. They found Alice Springs to be a real tourist town with many different dialects to be heard on the streets and in pubs.

Alice Springs was referred to as "the Alice" to locals. In fact throughout outback areas it was not uncommon to hear people talk about their visits to the

Curry, the Towers, the Isa or the Rock. It was "tough talk", it conserved energy and it automatically indicated you belonged in the outback.

Towards the end of 1975, Lindsay and Liz submitted their applications for transfer. Knowing their transfers were assured to a region of their choice, they took the liberty of applying for just one school—Nambour State High School. Their furniture was packed and removed and they boarded a plane for Brisbane, (all at the expense of the Department of Education). For Lindsay, the departing sight of the mine's smokestack was a pleasant farewell to a chapter of his life.

Nambour was one of the most favoured locations in Queensland. It was quite a large town thus having most of the amenities. Located on the Sunshine Coast, it was close to some of the best beaches, a great attraction after living in Mt Isa. Lindsay was familiar with the area having visited it several times in his youth. His grandparents lived in Nambour and his uncle had a farm at North Arm. In fact, his cousin Ray Turnbull had found him a house for them to rent before they arrived. Next year another cousin Bob Turnbull found them a property to buy. This property, as it turned out, was in Gold Creek Road, North Arm, not far from where his uncle's farm was located. The ten-acre property provided privacy and an opportunity to indulge in part-time farming—fruit trees, some cattle, fowls and sometimes pigs. Not all was cleared, particularly the area around a permanent creek, appropriately named Running Creek.

Accidents do happen! Sometimes they have diabolical outcomes. In 1979, Lindsay and Liz were returning from a holiday at Nowra, where Liz's brother Douglas was stationed as a helicopter pilot in the Navy. They had set out that morning from Narrabri to drive through Moree and then onto Inverell. The road was good, the driving conditions equally so, but not the incident soon to unfold. Lindsay was driving a short but safe distance behind another car. He would have overtaken it except that a car was coming from the other direction. Behind that car was another, the driver of which was evidently anxious to overtake the car he was following. Without checking, he attempted to overtake once the car in front of Lindsay had passed. They collided at point blank range! Both cars spun 180° and then rolled down an embankment. It was some time before Lindsay started to realise the situation they were in. They had left Narrabri with a full tank of petrol, and now he could smell it as it obviously leaked from the car. A gruff voice belonging to a truck driver, warned people not to light cigarettes or even come near the car. Lindsay looked over at Liz and saw the distress she was in. He asked the truck driver if he would get her out of the car, particularly because of the danger posed by the leaking petrol. In Lindsay's defence he made a quick decision without the time or presence of mind to think of other consequences. Liz had sustained dual fractures to her lower spine and should not have been moved by anyone without medical experience. But she was! Later, an ambulance took her to Moree Hospital.

Lindsay was firmly wedged in the car. His door would not open while the dashboard and some of the motor surrounded him. He had received superficial wounds to his face and a more serious wound to his right leg. The pain in his leg convinced him it was broken but that turned out not to be the case. As time elapsed, the blood from Lindsay's facial injuries gave the appearance of a seriously injured person to the point where one onlooker commented that, "I think he's gone"!

The fire brigade was summoned to cut open the car but wouldn't do so until Lindsay had been sedated with an injection of morphine. Then it was off to Moree Hospital. There his injuries were assessed as not major, were dressed and he was tucked up in a hospital bed.

There is a common phrase for the reaction of people to a major shock. This actually happened to Lindsay that night. When the nurse arrived in the morning to check on his progress, he was taking a shower. He was roundly chastised for getting up. Then she discovered the evidence on the bed!

Afterwards, he was taken around to see his wife. She was in traction as the x-rays showed fractures to the lower lumbar section of her spine. She had lost feeling (spinal cord shock) and was still unaware of what had happened. She was to be transported by plane to the Royal North Shore Hospital in Sydney.

Lindsay remained in hospital a few more days. He was interviewed by police to whom he could give accurate details of the accident. He was told that the other vehicle was driven by a man from Canberra (it was discovered later that he was a senior public servant), and that his passengers consisted of his wife and daughter. The daughter was seriously injured and was to be on the same plane to the same hospital as was Liz. Amongst other things, she had spinal fractures. The police also disclosed to Lindsay that he appeared to be the only person who could remember anything about the accident. Apparently neither of the cars behind whom the accident occurred, stopped. As he was walking up the corridor of the hospital he looked into one of the wards where a man looked sheepishly back. He was the other driver, and he remembered!

Having convinced the hospital doctor that he was well enough to leave and that, to reassure them further, he was going to stay at Inverell with his wife's parents, one of whom was a doctor and the other a nurse, Lindsay was discharged into their care.

Shortly after arriving in Inverell, Lindsay made arrangements to fly to Sydney to visit his wife. With bandages around his head and his right knee almost immobilised, he looked much worse than he was. On arrival in Sydney, Lindsay made his way to the hospital. It was, and probably still is, a very large hospital. Liz was still in the intensive care unit. She was able to talk to Lindsay and asked about the circumstances of the accident. After spending some hours there, Lindsay found the railway station and asked the station master about a train to Parramatta. Lindsay had made arrangements to stay with his aunt in North Mead, Parramatta. He was told the train would be arriving within the half-hour so bought a ticket. When the train arrived, there was no indication that it would take him to Parramatta. The station master assured him it would. As the train stopped at each station, Lindsay looked for the signs that indicated the name of the station. He also attempted to hear the station announcements. However, many of the announcers were either of ethnic origin or spoke incoherently. After many more stations, the train seemed to stop for an excessively long period of time. When a young couple boarded and settled into a seat opposite him, Lindsay enquired about when the train would arrive at Parramatta. Scarcely concealing their amusement, they informed him he was on the wrong line. This was the southern line and he should have changed trains at Granville. They were kind enough to alert him, on the return trip, when he was at Granville where he had little difficulty getting a train to Parramatta.

The instructions his aunt had given Lindsay was to catch a particular bus nearby the station, get out at a particular stop, and then walk the short distance to her house. There was no bus! Since it was now quite late, there probably wouldn't be one. So Lindsay decided to walk, having been shown the direction to North Mead. It was much further than he realised. When he finally knocked on his Aunt Thelma's door, she was aghast to see him with a bandaged head and with a right trouser leg considerably stained with blood. The stitches had loosened around the wound on his right knee. She thought Lindsay had been mugged, especially since it was around 11 pm.

Lindsay's Aunt Thelma was a real character. She had a sense of humour that surpassed any in her large family. But that night there was no indication of it. What she did indicate however, was that she retained her nursing skills. Lindsay was well fed whilst relating all the news. Finally, with the aid of a sleeping tablet, he was soon asleep.

The next day, Lindsay set off for the hospital armed with more instructions regarding public transport. The trip to the hospital went according to plan. The first thing Lindsay needed to do was to check in at Outpatients to get the stitches in his knee attended to. This done, he found Liz transferred to a ward. This was the start of a long and tedious stay in hospital for her. She could read but before too long, she was calling for the "lifters". Lifters were strong men whose job it was to turn patients who couldn't turn themselves. Since Liz was still suffering spinal shock, she needed to use their services. They weren't always on hand, sometimes being up to an hour away, or so Liz was told. When she was awake, she and Lindsay played cards or a dice game. When she slept, Lindsay wrote letters to home or to the staff at Nambour High School.

Then, when it was time to go, Lindsay followed the well-rehearsed track to the railway station. Now he was greeted by the station master, "Mr Parramatta" in his distinctly Italian dialect, "Here comes-a your train!"

After feeling much more confident about the train trip, Lindsay started to take more notice of what was inside the train. Before long, he noticed an amazing ability possessed by those who must surely be regular commuters. Their faces were mostly hidden behind their newspapers. As the train progressed from one station to the next, they continued, uninterrupted, to turn the pages as they read on. Then, when they had finished the last page, they folded up the newspaper, picked up their bag and walked to the door. The door opened and they disembarked. How did they do that? Finish the last page just as the train was stopping at their destination? And, they never looked out the window at all, as far as Lindsay could tell!

Eventually, it was time for Lindsay to return to Nambour. He had already missed two weeks of the second term. He hired a car at the expense, he was confident, of the insurer of the guilty party in the accident. From the school library, Lindsay borrowed a book entitled, "The Readers Digest Guide to Australian Family Law". Although he and Liz had engaged solicitors, Lindsay was determined to know everything for which he could claim. He kept a notepad in which telephone calls, fuel expenses and other such items were recorded. This turned out to be a lengthy process as Lindsay discovered, settlements of that nature are protracted affairs.

Soon, Liz was transferred to Inverell hospital. Her condition had stabilised and, fortunately, she had recovered the use of all parts of her body. Lindsay would drive down about every second weekend. On one occasion it was to show her the new car he had bought.

Then she was released from hospital to stay with her parents in Inverell. Lindsay continued to drive down to see her, a drive with which he became quite familiar. On one occasion, good friends Mal and Jean Lanham drove him down. On another occasion he drove down with his parents.

It was on one of these weekends, when he received a telephone call whilst at the hospital. It was shattering news—his cousin, Ray Turnbull, had died! Apparently, he was playing tennis when he collapsed suddenly and died of a massive heart attack. Since moving to Nambour, after Ray had organised accommodation for them, he and Lindsay had become close friends. They played cricket and tennis together. He was the most community-minded person that Lindsay had ever known. The previous season, Ray had captained their A Grade cricket team to win the premiership. It was just so unfair! He was only forty seven years of age.

After sick leave of almost a year, Liz was to return to work only to find she had been transferred to Burnside High School. How compassionate was the Department of Education? Furthermore, she discovered that, since she was the most senior physical education teacher there, she would have to write their programs of work. She did not enjoy that.

There were a few court cases after the accident. The other driver was charged with culpable driving. Lindsay gave his account of the accident. The other driver's legal representative had hired an expert who claimed there was evidence that the other car had braked sharply so that the driver lost control. Lindsay responded quite simply that that didn't happen. Since all others involved in the accident had claimed a loss of memory, the judge ignored the claim. In any case, there was no evidence to support the braking. He was committed to stand trial.

Liz and Lindsay drove down from Nambour to Moree for the District Court trial. They waited outside the courthouse for an eternity while a jury was empanelled. There must have been some preliminary discussions involving each legal team and the judge because eventually the news arrived that the case would not proceed. The police explained the situation to Lindsay and Liz. Neither was affected.

The settlement! After all the bills were paid, there was little remaining. It left Lindsay wondering what might have happened had they engaged a high profile legal team!

Nambour High School was one of Queensland's largest secondary schools with an enrolment of about one thousand two hundred students. As a rural high school, it incorporated a farm with a dairy, crops and fruit trees, allowing students to study agriculture, agricultural science, agricultural mechanics and animal husbandry. This attracted students from quite a distance away. The school had a reputation for high academic results. The teachers on staff were much older than Lindsay was accustomed to, but they were very experienced thus achieving the impressive academic results.

When he left Brisbane, his good friend, Bill Webb and some of his friends decided to take over renting the house that Lindsay and Peter were vacating. Bill was posted to Cooparoo High School as a maths/science teacher. After a year, he was transferred but chose not to accept it. He then started teaching at a private school.

Sometime later, another person came to share the board. He brought a greyhound with him to the house. Underneath was enclosed although the aged greyhound bitch looked as though she not only couldn't win a race but also probably wouldn't be capable of running away from 45 Amelia St. Bill, always the opportunist, started to take an interest in greyhound racing. His big chance soon came when the owner of this greyhound, Thor's Lisa, left (both the house and the dog). Bill investigated its pedigree and decided to breed from it. The first pups looked like champions but unfortunately died before getting to race.

By this time, Lindsay had completed two years in Mt Isa and was transferred to Nambour State High School. Bill sent the greyhound bitch to be mated with a notable sire called Early Copy. Bill had chosen the sire after studying the genealogy. A combination of their friendship, Lindsay's excitement about being involved in racing again, and the fact that he had ten acres where he lived, started a partnership between the two eventually involving many greyhounds. A likely prospect out of the several pups whelped was brought up to North Arm. Only the best of diets, veterinary care, as well as long walks/runs every morning saw this pup develop into a more than useful greyhound. All reports from the man who broke the dog in, (teaching it to chase a lure), were quite promising. The only thing that surprised him was that this greyhound, Jipco, wasn't interested in live kills at the end of trials (that he generally won easily). Jipco was given the racing name of Thor's Edition and sent to be trained by Mike O'Byrne, a leading trainer whom Bill had closely investigated. The dog became a champion, winning the Coca Cola Cup Final as second emergency. Later he won the Queensland Champion of Champions at the Gabba. From there, he went to Melbourne where he finished third in the National Championships. He won races at many tracks but was a favourite at the Gabba where he won many races in very fast times. Great memories and lots of fun (if no money to show for it)!

Lindsay continued his involvement in greyhound racing by building kennels on his property and gaining a trainers' licence. With the help of his neighbour, Brian, he cleared a short straight running track in the back paddock, complete with starting boxes and a drag lure. He had a few winners and a lot of interesting times, but the onset of a young family brought an end to this chapter of his life.

On arrival at Nambour High School, Lindsay was appointed Economics Co-ordinator, something which didn't go down well with the three teachers of that subject already there. His qualifications and experience in that position, albeit for only one year, probably got him the position. It was not a position of any great importance except that it helped improve Lindsay's confidence in a leadership role. This confidence led to numerous leadership positions, not much in his job as a teacher, but rather in other areas.

He became secretary then treasurer then president of the Nambour Cricket Club. He became senior vice-president, a selector and a member of the management committee of the Sunshine Coast Cricket Association. After serving as a representative of the Coast Cricket Association on the Sunshine Coast/Gympie Zone Council, he later became secretary/ treasurer of that organisation. Lindsay captained Nambour in first, second and third divisions as well as the Sunshine Coast Seconds. As a member of Yandina Tennis Club, he was vice-president and later honorary auditor. When Lindsay's children attended North Arm Primary School, he served as treasurer and later president of the Parents and Citizens' Association. He coached the Sunshine Coast 15 year's Cricket team for about thirteen years and the Nambour junior cricket teams in which his two sons, Greg and John played. Lindsay had the pleasure of winning two State Championships as coach of the Sunshine Coast team, one quite memorable since Greg played in that team. For cricket championships held on the Sunshine Coast, Lindsay convened two Primary Schools Carnivals, two under 15 year's Carnivals, two Open Schoolboys' Carnivals and two National Carnivals.

He also won the Under 16 Premiership in his last year of coaching, a team of which his son John was a member. Three times he was awarded the Sunshine Coast Junior Coach of the year. Lindsay was awarded life membership of the Nambour Cricket Club, Queensland Secondary Schools Cricket and the Antiquarians Cricket Club.

In the late 1980's, Keith Lees who had played cricket at Warwick and later moved to the Sunshine Coast, organised through a chain of contacts, a team of players in an advanced stage of their cricket careers. Most had played at a high level and consequently had not lost their competitive edge although some of their cricketing ability had waned. Matches were organised on an irregular basis against a growing number of similar teams.

The highlight of the season (generally the off-season of Club Cricket) was the September trip to Jondaryn. Greg Sprott was, years before, a very good player in Toowoomba and had played against Lindsay's father. He gathered a group of players from around that district to play against the Antiquarians, as Peter Gilroy had suggested this Sunshine Coast team be named. The country hospitality was never more evident than on the day of the very first trip. The Jondaryn cricket ground was a converted paddock that grew mainly prickles and had a concrete pitch in the centre. An ex-school room was moved there to serve as a clubhouse. Yet inside, on that first trip, were warm scones and cream to eat with a cup of tea. Lunch was a generous BBQ which the locals provided. At the conclusion of the game, all players adjourned to the local pub where the hospitality continued and other non-playing locals were engaged in conversation of great interest, considering their different existence. A similar trip happened each year and it was rarely difficult to get a full complement of Antiquarians on the bus.

Other games against University Old Boys, Bundaberg, I Zingarees, Kingaroy, the Wanderers, Maryborough, Valleys Old Boys, the Queensland Cricketers Club and Beenleigh to name most, had one thing in common—they were played in a serious manner with no player prepared to embarrass himself. Yet the competitiveness was restrained during the game and forgotten immediately afterwards. Over a drink, stories, sometimes embellished, of past cricket incidents were exchanged among players of both sides.

As Nambour and the Sunshine Coast experienced rapid population growth, the school exceeded its capacity after reaching an enrolment of one thousand four hundred students. Lindsay was one of a deputation of five teachers who met with the Minister for Education to lobby for another school to be built in the vicinity. Eventually, Burnside High School was opened in Nambour and later still, Coolum High School drew quite a large number of students from Nambour High School. Despite this, enrolment numbers remained above one thousand, always well in excess of Burnside High School. By the 1990's, many private schools began operating on the Sunshine Coast. Nevertheless, enrolments at

Nambour remained at capacity requiring an indoor sports centre and a technology centre to be built.

Lindsay was not a qualified auditor but a combination of many years as treasurer of organisations plus qualifications in both Economics and Maths made it possible for him to provide his services free of charge to local organisations. It required approval by the Auditor-Generals Department. His decision to help in this respect was prompted by the considerable fees charged by registered auditors to organisations who simply didn't have the funds to pay. Over about twenty years, Lindsay audited accounts for the local rural fire boards, the Yandina Tennis Club, the North Arm State School Parents and Citizens' Association, the North Arm Hall Committee, and the North Arm School.

All four children of Lindsay and Liz completed their primary schooling at North Arm State School, and their secondary schooling at Nambour State High School. Fiona completed a Science Degree at the University of Queensland followed by a Master's Degree in Dietetics at Griffiths University. She obtained a job at Frankston Hospital. Fiona also operates a private clinic. Almost a true Melburnian now, she and her partner, Jim, have built a house at Mt Martha on the Mornington Peninsula. Fiona was also very good at a wide range of sports including gymnastics in which she won Queensland titles and competed in two international competitions; athletics in which she competed in Queensland Championships every year; volleyball in which she represented Nambour High School in the State finals; and vigoro in which she represented the Sunshine Coast in the Queensland Championships. One year she won a tennis premiership in a team that included her father. Fiona had a determination to succeed as much as any person could have.

Bronwyn, perhaps because she was so close in age to Fiona (nineteen months younger), chose a different course. Bronwyn had sporting talent but without a competitive attitude. She graduated from a modelling course and pursued a career in hospitality. After working in this industry at Caloundra, Uluru and Sydney, she accepted an opportunity in a new industry as a DVD editor.

Greg and John both achieved well throughout their primary schooling with Greg proceeding through high school with a minimum of work. He had, like his father, the experience of being taught by *his* father. Greg didn't complete Year 12. He had clearly been through such a traumatic experience that he wanted to leave home and start working. In this respect, he was lucky to get a job with his uncle, Peter Kelly, and his partner in the business, Dave. They both had a very positive influence on Greg's development. A few years later, Greg spent six months working in a ski resort in Canada. On his return, Greg began a new career in marketing. He approached this with great gusto often working seven days a week. The business built up rapidly. However, the desire to get out of Brisbane and back to the Sunshine Coast caused him to change jobs and become a carpet-cleaner. Greg is an avid sports enthusiast and player, particularly of cricket and soccer.

John, the youngest, completed a degree in exercise physiology. He is also a talented sportsman especially in cricket, soccer, athletics and tennis. John is quite extroverted although he tends to have long relationships with few girlfriends. His girlfriend, Jess, is very industrious, intelligent and organises John well. He was able to gain a scholarship to study in Michigan, USA.

Lindsay saw no reason to leave Nambour High School. As his years there passed, he was allocated to better classes—for Lindsay, better meant more academic and more senior classes. A major change in his career came in 1998 when a deputy principal, Darren Edwards, approached Lindsay about becoming Year Level Co-ordinator for the Year 9's. Accepting that position required him, amongst other things, to conduct an assembly each week. It was with great preparation, yet trepidation, that Lindsay took charge of his first assembly. Gradually, however, this role improved his communication and discipline skills, as well as involving Lindsay in more administrative matters in the school. The confidence this provided contributed largely to his acceptance of positions of Acting Head of Department in Maths and Physical Education. In 2000, the resignation of the Maths Head of Department prompted Lindsay to apply for the position. He found the whole process difficult to deal with and eventually missed out on the position.

A tradition began not long after Peter met Jill. Each year on the Queen's Birthday long weekend, they would go fishing. This progressed to the stage where it became a houseboat holiday. They hired a houseboat from Tin Can Bay. Generally, there was another person invited, usually a business acquaintance or friend of Peter. They made their way out of the Bay to the Great Sandy Straits. Most of the time was spent fishing or crabbing.

One particular year they ventured up to Garry's Anchorage in perfect weather, with Dave Johnson the third of the crew. Peter was driving while Lindsay and Dave were enjoying the sun up on the bow of the boat. Suddenly, Dave jumped overboard. As the boat passed him, he grabbed hold of the dinghy which they were towing, climbed in, and then, with a running jump, landed on the back stairs of the houseboat. What a trick! Lindsay was sure, he could do it too. So in he went, caught the dinghy, but failed in his attempt to jump back on the houseboat. So, as the houseboat continued on, Dave untied the dinghy. Lindsay swam to it, climbed in, started the motor and caught up with the houseboat again. Despite the cold, much time was spent in the water that weekend.

Each November, with a group of people, Lindsay drove to Brisbane for the First Test of the summer. They were members of the Queensland Cricketers Club, or at least had guest passes to use the Club. The Club is located at the Gabba and offers reasonably good facilities. Previous to its present location, it was behind the wicket thus offering the best viewing position on the ground.

The group stayed in a nearby hotel. The accommodation didn't rate many stars but was ideal for their purpose. They had a routine apart from the cricket which included a visit to the German Club on the Saturday night, a curry in one of the many restaurants in the vicinity and usually a meal in the "Aussie Nash". Other incidents came under the category, "What happens on tour stays on tour".

Lindsay continued his involvement in sport, especially cricket. He played for the Nambour Cricket Club and in representative cricket until he was fifty. Although quite an ordinary player, he captained Nambour to win five of his seven premierships. He also captained the Sunshine Coast Seconds cricket team for four years without suffering a defeat. Although he was more talented in other sports, cricket became his favourite sport. Tennis was also one of Lindsay's popular sports. In fact his whole family played tennis so that even during a hot summer's holiday, they often hired a court to play. Lindsay enjoyed Veterans' Tennis. It was friendly while being quite competitive. In fact, Lindsay, playing for Yandina, played against his sister, Jill, who played for Burpengary.

When he turned fifty, Lindsay had a party in the North Arm Hall. Guests came in costumes depicting sportspeople. Grant painted himself black to resemble a Sri Lankan cricketer. Peter had obviously gone to a lot of trouble to kit himself out as a sky jumper. Even Lindsay's father joined the occasion by wearing a Greg Norman hat and carrying a golf club. Lindsay was dressed as W.G. Grace who was also still playing cricket at age fifty, albeit First Class cricket. It was a memorable night.

Lindsay was about three weeks older than his good friend Pat. Pat was also a teacher at Nambour High School. Shortly after both had reached the age of fifty, Lindsay remarked to Pat that he was not, "Going into the nervous fives". The expression, using a cricketing description of a batsman progressing nervously from ninety runs to his century, referred to their nearness to retirement at age fifty-five.

Using his wildest imagination, Lindsay could not have anticipated how those five years would have been spent.

A Man in a Wheelchair

I lay on the ground thinking how lucky I was to have survived the fall without breaking anything. But why hadn't my legs reached the ground? It must have been an odd sight to see me lying there with my feet in the air. I felt no pain whatsoever but something must have directed me to seek help. I asked John to ring the ambulance and get Mum down here. I don't remember how John reacted, but it seemed no time at all before the ambulance arrived. When Liz came to help me, the more she tried to calm me, the more agitated I became, unable to get enough air into my lungs. I had always known how competent she was in emergencies, but at that time it didn't matter. *I couldn't breathe and, as a result, I was going to die!* Then I was given oxygen. I could breathe now and started to take in some of what was happening around me. Nobody was talking to me, just to each other! Very soon, I heard the helicopter. It seemed ages before it landed. The paramedics went to work—strapped me to a stretcher and put me in the helicopter. Still I wasn't told what was wrong with me that seemed to be so important that I was being airlifted to hospital. Then I heard the answer to one of Liz's questions—45 minutes to the Princess Alexandra Hospital in Brisbane! Why not Nambour Hospital? It is quite large catering for all types of injuries and illnesses. Now if only I could keep breathing for 45 minutes, I would be alright.

During all this time, I was conscious and taking in most things in a reasonably calm way. But it was hardly reasonable when I said to Greg, "I think this is it!" What a foolish thing to say, and many times since then, I have regretted saying it.

Still I had no idea of my injuries, my paralysis—just that something was wrong! I knew nothing about spinal cord injuries. I had seen people in wheelchairs but I didn't know they might have been paraplegic or quadriplegic. And, all the time the ambulance officers fussed about something!

I had always wanted to ride in a helicopter. But this ride wasn't fun. I knew I had to concentrate on breathing—*breathe for forty five minutes and I'll be in hospital and whatever was wrong would be put right!* I was starting to feel pain now. The flight was so bumpy!

When I was admitted to the acute care ward, I remember only pain. How many times did a medical person have to push a pin into me? Up and down the length of my body saying, "Can you feel this?" I was so thirsty but they wouldn't give me a drink! "Suck on this ice cube"—"Please, can I have a drink?"—"Soon, when things settle down"! Perhaps they thought that if I suffered so much from thirst, I wouldn't feel my injuries. The pain in my stomach was so bad I couldn't bear to have anyone touch it. X-rays after x-rays! Questions about where it hurt until all my body hurt. It was so hot and I just had to have a drink! Someone tried to push a tube through my nostrils—I pulled it out, it was pushed back in—I pulled it out again! When would this person realise it is impossible to put a tube down my nose? He had obviously experienced this before because he didn't get angry with me. He also had another tactic—dipping the tube in morphine so that I felt nothing. Now I was beginning to take it all in! *This must be serious!*

I realised much later that, although it was very unpleasant, the tube did serve a useful purpose. Then at last, it was just a nurse and me. She was so good. She would give me a little water as well as the ice. Still, I didn't realise the extent of my injuries or the paralysis! How do you know when you have paralysis if you can't feel it?

That night they operated to open my stomach and see what was causing the pain. There seemed to be some damage there but the medical people didn't appear to be too concerned. I had more time with that splendid nurse but it ended when they came to take me across to the Spinal Ward, whenever that was.

Sometime during the next 24 hours, I was visited by Dr Bill Davies. He told me all about my injuries but I didn't take much in. I was getting constant attention from the nurses. I was aware of my surroundings. I was attached to drips and I still had the tube in my nose. In my hand was a plunger connected to another bag on the stand. A nurse told me that if I had any pain I just needed to push the plunger and it would inject morphine. How marvellous that turned out to be! If I lost that plunger during the night, I would be so alarmed that I would call out for a nurse to find it for me. The only other thing that woke me was when I accidentally touched the paralysed part of my body. That part under the covers was like a large hunk of meat placed there for some reason. During morning baths, I washed down to the level of my paralysis and waited for a nurse to wash the rest. Before long, with all the sympathy they could muster, the nurses told me to, "Get used to it", so I had to wash down as far as I could reach. It wasn't a pleasant experience. In fact using a washer for baths, day after day for six weeks didn't make me feel good about my personal hygiene. The part that was most difficult was shaving. After lathering my face, the pillow and bedclothes, I stared into a convex mirror mounted on a stand (the type of mirror used in places so that one could look around, over and under things). Then with a razor dipped in tepid bath water, I removed about half of my whiskers. I was desperate for a shampoo. Eventually a nurse, kind enough to oblige, was rostered on one weekend.

Then one day, as I stared at nothing in particular, it suddenly dawned on me that I might be incurring considerable medical expenses. I had private health insurance but it covered me for only general hospitalisation. Later I found that my private insurance covered me for nothing—not for wheelchairs or any other medical aids that I would need. And, the hospitalisation was free!

I was on a bed that tilted from side to side. Every four hours I had to change. The procedure became familiar. First, the nurses would remove the tray from beside my bed. Then they asked me to inject some morphine. I was hooked on it! A couple of nurses held me while the bed was hydraulically tilted about $30°$, alternating between the left side, horizontal, and the right side. How I loved the horizontal! I could go to sleep there, do a crossword, or read a book. Lying on my side was painful, especially the left side when my shoulder hurt. Perhaps I landed on my shoulder during the fall. Pillows were placed in position then the nurses left, usually leaving my tray out of reach and on the wrong side of the bed. It contained my book, the newspaper, the radio, the mobile phone, my water and other essentials. They seemed inconvenienced when I called them back.

Later when I was using the bathroom in a shower chair, I used to take two cakes of soap to the shower in case I dropped one. I thought it preferable to calling a nurse to pick up a cake of soap and I certainly couldn't do it myself.

I remember a young male nurse who may have been working on probation. When he attended to anything I needed, he would never leave without asking, "Is there anything else I can do for you?" I also remember when, one day, he came to give me my injection he enquired, "Would you like the needle in your stomach or in your leg?" Like most people, I don't like needles! Each day I had two Hepron needles to prevent Deep Vein Thrombosis (since I was immobilised). The needles were always given to me in my stomach. If I was lucky, it was below the level of my injury (so I didn't feel it). But to have it in my leg would be wonderful! I wished I had found out about this earlier in my six-week confinement.

How often I called out for nurses to tilt the bed back up before the four hours had elapsed—some would, some wouldn't and some would give me a lecture about the importance of keeping to the schedule. As if I needed to hear it again! The bed was also fitted with a machine that sent pulses through my legs to provide some circulation.

During his second or third visit, Dr Davies explained what the meeting of doctors had decided to do. It seemed that, after fracturing and obviously damaging the spinal cord, the spine had moved back into alignment. Therefore, the fracture would repair itself by calcifying over if I was immobilised for six weeks. Immobilised! I could move only my arms anyway (something which I later discovered was a blessing, witnessing the predicament of quadriplegics). How I counted down those six weeks! The doctor seemed surprised when I could instantly remind him how long I had been in that state. Constantly I thought that if, after six weeks, the bones hadn't mended, an operation would be necessary. Then I would have to spend more time confined to bed.

Gradually all the connections were removed. First, the tube in my nose! Its removal was nowhere near as uncomfortable as its insertion! Then the morphine supply was removed. What a sad parting! I had to convince myself that it was a sign of progress. Finally, the saline drip was taken out. The welcome result of this last event was that I could start eating again—one of my great passions in life. The procedure—*liquids only, soft foods,* then at last I was *normal foods*—normal hospital food! The pleasure soon wore off. Monday lunch (ham with salad), evening (lasagne—cooked the hospital way), Tuesday lunch (silverside with salad), evening (roast lamb with vegetables), Wednesday lunch (cold roast lamb with salad), evening (roast beef with vegetables), Thursday lunch (cold roast beef with salad), evening (roast pork with vegetables), Friday lunch (cold roast pork with salad), evening (fish and chips), Saturday lunch (cold meat with salad), evening (pie with vegetables), Sunday lunch (cold meat with salad), evening (spaghetti bolognaise—the bland edition). Many of the younger male patients would look in to see what was for dinner, then wheel out, call a taxi and go to the local RSL. Then sometimes the word would get around that the "Chef's Special" was on. Everyone was in for that because it *was* good. Otherwise, the pizza delivery boy knew all the patients and their beds in the Unit.

Shortly after admission, I was presented with a booklet entitled, "Spinal Cord Injuries". I asked a nurse to put it at the back of the bottom drawer. I refused to even consider the notion that I wouldn't recover soon.

One day a man was brought in following a water skiing accident in which he apparently skied into the bank at considerable speed. He had a fractured spine but no spinal cord injury. He was immediately transferred to another hospital—those spinal unit beds were at a premium and he simply didn't qualify!

After about two weeks, I summoned up the courage to ask the doctor how long I might have to wait before recovery from the paralysis began to happen. "Six to sixty days". Sixty days was ages away! I felt much better.

Then one day I saw my leg move. Oh what boundless joy! I couldn't wait to tell Dr Davies. "That was a spasm. They will probably start to increase now. I will put you on some medication for that." More medicine needed when I was clearly recovering—that made no sense at all! I think he realised then that I hadn't read the book or at least the chapter on *spasticity*. So he patiently explained how muscles could spasm although no recovery from paralysis was happening. "Everyone is different. There is no way of knowing whether recovery is happening." This and subsequent statements by nurses, physiotherapists, occupational therapists, G.P.'s and other medical people made me realise the conspiracy not to give any hope, false or otherwise, was a major factor in my treatment.

Wattie was in the bed next to me. On her 40th birthday, the hospital staff decorated her bedside with balloons (inflated condoms) and anything else that looked celebratory. I don't remember anything like a cake, but that was probably fortuitous since I was still on a liquid diet. Lying on my back made it very difficult to exchange pleasantries with the other patients. I would sense their presence and extend greetings without making eye contact. This is how I said, "Happy Birthday"; to a person I hadn't really seen. Wattie was generally very pleasant, but one day she gave the nurses a half-hour outburst, full of accusations and profanities that made me feel uncomfortable. She had been in the Spinal unit for some time, and I later realised how frustration could boil over to the extent that an incident like this could easily occur.

One night I heard the fire alarm go off (while we were still on the seventh floor of the old hospital). Before long, I could hear the approaching siren of a fire engine. Apparently, a fire had started on one of the vacated floors below, but it worried me enough to ask a nurse how I would be evacuated, given that I had an unstabilised fracture. Apparently, there was a chute somewhere that I would have to slide down on a mattress. I never needed to use it.

WEEK 6 had at last passed. I was expecting to have an x-ray immediately after breakfast, and news, good or otherwise, before lunch. The day dragged on; the doctor visited and I immediately reminded him that the six weeks had transpired. He seemed surprised—something

like, "Is it already?" He arranged for an x-ray for the next day. I didn't
fancy x-rays, particularly this one that might deliver bad news. Because
of my unstabilised fracture, I had to be hoisted up while the plate was
inserted under my spine. Then there was always 'just one more'. I always
imagined that during the six weeks the bones either side of my fracture
were being calcified over to heal the fracture. Apparently, the bones had
to grow together again. I knew that young people's bones grew but did
this still happen when a person was 50? If so, I would be left with a large
calcified lump. That's what it felt like when I was lowered onto the x-ray
plate—and how it hurt!

After that, I had to wait for the Wednesday meeting of specialists when
they considered the progress of all spinal patients. I spent the morning
staring at the newspaper but focussed only on the possible sound of Dr
Davies' walking cane approaching. Sometime after lunch, he approached
accompanied by another person who looked like he possessed abundant
medical knowledge. I had a dread feeling they were going to explain
the procedures necessary to fix my back since the x-ray showed the plan
for it to heal over unaided had not been successful. Instead, Dr Davies
introduced me to a urinary specialist. He explained to me the process
of changing from using an in-dwelling catheter to self-catheterisation. I
was polite enough to hear him out, but at last I got a chance to address
Dr Davies, "What about the x-rays? Has my fracture mended?". "Oh, it's
OK". After six weeks, there should have been balloons and champagne!

During those six weeks, I received wonderful support from family
and friends. Liz arrived about an hour after I went into Acute Care. She
visited three times each week and more often on school holidays. As well,
she was managing the household including Bronwyn, Greg and John, the
latter two both still at school. I used to watch the minute hand travelling
endlessly around the dial of the clock, (the clock that Therese had sent
me that was the trophy for winning the Veterans' Tennis Competition).
At other times, I studied the ceiling or composed letters (in which I tried
to include something amusing to suggest to the recipients that I was far
from depressed).

Each of my two Year 12 classes had sent cards to me. When I replied, I told one
of my classes that the ceiling consisted of squares about one metre square and that a
light was placed in such a position that the distance from the light to the furtherest
corner of the square seemed to be the same as the length of the side of the square.
I asked them to calculate the distance that the light was from the nearest corner. I
had spent a lot of time looking at that ceiling! To the other class I told them that
my stay in the hospital depended on how quickly I became rehabilitated and that
my rehabilitation depended on how hard I worked in the gym. I challenged them
to use their knowledge of composite functions to give me a function that would

determine when I would be discharged, and that I would post this function up on the wall of the gym beside the photo of Arnold Schwarzenegger. I didn't get a reply from either. Was that a sad reflection on my teaching? The Maths staff however did send me a card and a gift of a special pen that apparently would continue to operate under any conditions. I told them that it certainly wrote while I was lying on my back and that it continued to work even after I dunked it in my water bowl, but I couldn't yet verify that it would still write in outer space. Now I know that it does stop working when it runs out of ink.

When I was first hoisted out of bed, the scales on the hoist measured my weight as 62kg. I had lost 24 kg during the six weeks on the bed. I was placed in a chair and encouraged to do some reading. It was a weird sensation! I did try some reading but I soon needed to lie down again. These daily and then twice-daily routines continued for the next week. After that, I made my way to the gym where I started using half-kilogram weights. Up to this point I was being supervised by a very competent trainee physiotherapist, Amelia. In her last semester of study, she was required to complete a number of six-week practicals at various hospitals in various wards.

Each day a lot of mail arrived—mostly *Get Well Cards.* Those from Nambour High School were inscribed with so many messages from staff members that it was touching to think that so many people still thought about me despite the hectic pace that is the norm of nearly every school day. Cards and letters came from students, past and present, as well as friends and relatives as the news spread. How I enjoyed reading and rereading them! My sister Jill visited often. She was always very positive, had lots of news and made a habit of plastering these cards on the surrounding walls, windows and cupboards. It made my corner of the ward very colourful and pleasant. I even had photos of all the boys in the cricket team that I had been coaching. One nurse whose name I won't mention asked if they were my children. *What's the name for eleven children of the same age?*

Then there were the other visitors. How I remember the visits by my parents, particularly in the early days when it was very hot and they hadn't discovered the shortcut from the railway station so they walked up that steep hill beside the hospital. Dad always had a quiz or similar that he left with me as they were leaving. Later they would accompany me to the gym and help, or provide encouragement, as I went through my daily tortures. We conversed on the telephone twice each week. Past students, tennis players (Peter and Des), many teachers as well as friends visited. Mal Sprott who was manager of the Sunshine Coast Schoolboys' teams while I was the coach visited regularly. So also did Bill Webb and Bob Murphy. Fred Hatchman, whose daughter was also in the Spinal

Unit, invariably dropped by to say hello and have a chat. The school chaplain, Ros, visited often. She and many of her friends prayed for me, which was a touching thought. When Cheryl visited, she brought me, amongst other things, a cricket bat. It was the one her son Kobi had been using when, at a schoolboys' carnival, I advised him it was too heavy. It became my "visitor's book".

One day I saw a man with a distinctive swagger and who looked very much like my cousin, Michael Glover, walking in the direction of my bed. Michael had flown up from Sydney as soon as he heard the news. We were close cousins, (still are), of the same age with children of similar ages, but a gesture like that was staggering. I had numerous visits from my school colleagues, family friends, past and present students and teachers involved in schoolboys' cricket.

Then one day Grant Ledger came to visit with sons, Steven and Michael. He told me that he was going to organise a charity golf day to raise funds for me, particularly to make all the necessary modifications to our house. When Grant says he will do something, you have to believe him, even a project such as this which I thought, at the very least, would be difficult. Enlisting the help of Pat Drew, the Nambour Cricket Club, Nambour High School and many tradesmen, Grant organised the golf day, a raffle and an auction. I was allowed to leave hospital for the day to attend the most overwhelming event I have ever experienced. Players from all cricket clubs on the Coast, teachers from many schools, Peter and Dave, friends and members of the golf club turned up to play golf or bid on some of the priceless sporting memorabilia, (like Ashley Noffke's playing shirt signed by all team members of Queensland's successful Pura Cup team of 2002, a football jersey signed by Arthur Beetson, and a collector's print of Queensland's first winner of the Golden Slipper Stakes), on auction. However, the sight of my very good friend, Bob Polzin, arriving, straight from hospital, carrying an intravenous drip and looking a shadow of the immensely strong plasterer with whom I often shared a few beers was the over-riding indication of the significance of the day.

The end of the six-week healing process marked the beginning of my rehabilitation. It was constantly emphasised that I was being prepared to live the rest of my life in a wheelchair. The Spinal Unit seemed increasingly a jail from which I would be released only when I passed all the tests. Even then, I would be on eternal probation. The problem was that as I passed one test, another more difficult test awaited. I think that physiotherapists continue to, "Move the goalposts", so that the patient can never kick the winning goal. At the end of a session when I was looking forward to lunch, Brooke invariably decided we should do the, "transferring from the wheelchair to a lounge chair and back again", routine. I did not look forward to this since I simply couldn't manage it, (and anyway I couldn't ever imagine why I would want to do it, especially a lounge chair on which all the springs had collapsed so that I might as well have been on the floor). Later they did ease me onto the floor to teach me strategies to get back into the chair, none of which worked. I suggested alternative strategies like crying loudly until people came to help me. Since leaving the Unit, I have experienced many falls and this last strategy has always worked.

I obtained a licence to drive a vehicle modified by installing hand controls. This required some lessons with a driving school suitably equipped. My second lesson was in the rain immediately after I had just experienced my first fall from a wheelchair.

I was waiting in the gym for my physio to hoist me onto a mat to start stretching. Since Brooke seemed to be busy, I decided to try to transfer directly from my wheelchair. I had seen plenty of people do it and I had done it with the help of a slideboard and a supervisor. I was virtually there when a spasm caused me to slip off the edge of the mat. It was an eerie experience to slide helplessly down to the floor, land on my knees then on to my side virtually feeling nothing—certainly no pain whatsoever. When I attempted this feat, there were very few people in the gym. Now they appeared from everywhere as I was roundly scolded by my physio—in fact, there was very little sympathy from anyone. I thought someone might have at least acknowledged my brave attempt.

To drive in the city was challenging enough *before my accident.* To do it while getting used to hand controls was an experience I never wished to repeat. Embarrassingly, the most frequent rebukes from the instructor, (who was not inclined to rebuke), were my traffic infringements that had nothing to do with my disability. Later in my rehabilitation a physio showed me how to transfer into the driver's seat then reach out, disassemble the wheelchair and place the parts in the car before driving off. By doing this I was completely independent if I wished to drive somewhere. However, it became so difficult that I drove less frequently as time went by.

I was also expected to use the kitchen. The occupational therapist, Glenda, rostered me on with two other younger men whose choice it was to cook some pizzas. I followed instructions obediently and before too long, two delicious pizzas emerged from the oven. Eating them was a skill I had acquired over many years and came back to me quite quickly. I hoped no one asked me to cook one again.

There was a diverse group of patients in the unit. Paul was a quadriplegic whose only visitor was his solicitor. Yet, he sat outside the lifts and watched everyone arrive and depart. Some would stay in bed all day defying all attempts by physios and nurses to get them to do some repatriation. Older people seemed to be waiting only for a carer and a place to live. Others, like Allan Cowie, were highly motivated, soon regaining their strength and the necessary skills to make an early departure (recovery is something that doesn't occur in the Spinal Unit such as it might in other parts of the hospital).

Allan was a highly successful jockey. Sadly, he had a fall in a race at an important meeting. I had seen the fall on a news bulletin prior to my accident. So he entered the Spinal Unit a few weeks before me. I was inspired by Allan, his positive attitude and quick adjustment. I think he amazed everyone, patients and staff, when one day he demonstrated how he could get out of his chair, onto the floor and then back up again. On another occasion, he pulled himself up a short flight of stairs and then flopped back down the stairs again. Later I thought, despite all these skills, he would never get back on a horse again, whereas, I could go back into a classroom.

Gym routine was much the same each day. First there was a set of stretching exercises followed by strengthening work and finally skills training. The latter was sometimes interesting when I would be required to catch or hit a balloon without overbalancing. Later it became a basketball then a medicine ball. On one occasion Brooke asked me to throw quoits at a peg or throw balls into a basket. All of these things I could do quite well, but only because of my sporting prowess. In the gym, it was the practice that everyone was encouraged in whatever they did by each of the other patients. It was something we all needed. One elderly woman, despite all the encouragement, battled to make any progress. In fact, as she pushed her wheelchair slowly along towards an automatic door, it would open but then close before she could get through it. So she would wait patiently for someone to come to her assistance.

Rhonda surprised us all one day when, on the gym mat opposite me, she showed her physio that she could lift her left leg, and then her right leg. The physio, very surprised, said," How long have you been able to do this?" "I don't know!" Then there was Billy. Billy, a young man in his early twenties, was a quadriplegic with injuries so severe that he needed help with everything. Most of the time he spent in bed, but it wasn't unproductive because he wrote by manipulating a pen in his mouth. He wrote a book and had begun to write poetry.

Some of us sat out on the veranda after gym waiting for dinner. We would comment on the progress made that day in demolishing the old hospital, or speculate on what the new earthworks were for. None of us ever talked about our troubles or about anything to do with spinal cord injuries. Yet, after I was home for some time, I craved the company of other paras to compare notes.

One night with a group of other patients, I took a taxi down to the local RSL Club to watch the State of Origin match. Although we expected to be there only a couple of hours, I took three catheters, (normally enough for twelve hours), with me. We had a delicious meal and a few beers before the match started. I had not had a beer since my admission. I tried to work out, by remembering my pre-accident days in pubs, how long I would normally have waited before I had to visit the toilet. After this calculation, I subtracted an hour and went to the toilet to find there was very little need. Later, I remembered that, after the first visit, the next visit came sooner. Anyway, I should go before the start of the game! Two catheters gone without much return! I considered watching the game without drinking but that seemed unrealistic. At half time, guess what I did? I don't know whether it was the worry about a bladder accident or Queensland's impending comprehensive defeat that reduced my enjoyment of the second half, but I was pleased when the taxis arrived to take us back.

The final step before leaving the Unit was to sleep in a double bed. This required me to do my own turns during the night, wake myself to catheterise, get myself into and out of bed, shower and use the toilet independently and dress myself. I rather muddled my way through this, thinking I must have impressed someone important because I was nearing my exit from hospital. On reflection, there must have been such a long waiting list that what I did was enough and it was time to give up my bed.

At last I was given a date for my discharge. All at once, there were so many things to be done. What wheelchair would I order? (There were so many different types, which were apparently different, but whose difference I couldn't detect.) Who would pay for it? How much would it cost me? How long would I wait until it was built? What would I do in the meantime? What about the shower chair? I found out about C.A.S.S. (the Continence Aid Subsidy Scheme). An order was placed for me. I had to wheel across to the main hospital to collect a host of prescription drugs.

Liz started to take some of my possessions home, although I was not finished in Brisbane yet. Three large boxes of books, all the cards and letters I had received plus odds and ends were taken home to North Arm. Then I moved to Coopers Plains where a house, owned by the Princess Alexandra Hospital, was a dedicated place for spinal injury patients to live for a time under a Transitional Repatriation Program. During the first week, I lived there with Liz and John for company and assistance. My second week there was spent with Bronwyn, while the next week I had Fiona for company although she was not to assist me in any significant way. In any case, she was starting her Master's Degree and so was either at university or studying during that time. I didn't stay for the fourth week. Apparently that was not normally the problem. Some patients were difficult to move on.

During my stay there, I was visited by a physiotherapist, a social worker and an occupational therapist. Each of these was excellent help, I suppose because for the first time, I could see the imminence of living in my home and the problems I would encounter. One of these problems, (which was not planned), occurred when I tipped out of my shower chair while trying to reach the washer that I had dropped. Liz and John were there to help me then. That set me wondering what I would have done should they not have been there. Crying out very loudly would not have worked. I decided that I would have pushed the wheelchair in front of me as I moved my bottom along the floor towards the lounge room. In the lounge room was a three-seater lounge chair. If I removed one of the cushions, placed it suitably on the floor, I could lift my bottom onto that cushion. From there, I would transfer up onto a stack of two cushions, then up onto the part of the chair without a cushion. I would transfer sideways on the lounge chair from no cushion to one to two and then back into the wheelchair. It took me about 15 minutes to construct the plan. I expect it would have taken much longer to do it (if I could). And my Maths' students wondered why I emphasised problem solving so much!

There were times when I enjoyed being alone in the house. This allowed me to listen to music, do the crosswords and, of course, all the household chores. I never became depressed—I had too much to plan. My life was going down a path vastly different to the one I had mapped out. Could I return to live at North Arm—in a high-set house on ten acres? What would teaching be like in a wheelchair? Or cricket coaching? What would I do in retirement? How would I be affected financially?

After about six months in Brisbane, I returned home. I was visited again by Trish Nolan who wanted to be sure that I still wanted to return to teaching. I was sure. She explained how a "graduated return to work" program operated. I remember the first day I went back to Nambour High School. I was fortunate that two rooms at ground level had become available. Previously they had been used by the Special Needs Unit of the school. This Unit had outgrown the area and were moving to new premises. An additional bonus was the accessible toilet attached to one of the rooms. Some modifications were made to the room that was to become my classroom. The other room, quite large having previously been a classroom, was initially occupied by only two of us.

I was introduced to Nicky who had a contract to take my classes. She was very friendly and extremely competent. The students were reserved, curious but very interested when I spoke to them about my medical condition.

Telling students about my medical condition left me open to criticism of a desire to elicit sympathy. However, I knew how interested students would be to see a person who many had not seen before, assigned to teach them Mathematics.

After all, sitting in a wheelchair highlighted my disability. I also recalled that, before my accident, I knew nothing about the circumstances associated with being paraplegic. But sitting in a wheelchair indicates only my inability to walk. So I told the students about the thoracic part of the spine, about the spinal cord and how the level of the injury caused the body parts below that level to shut down. This meant I had lost control over things like my bladder and bowel. I explained that incontinence could be the greatest problem in public and in the classroom. They were intrigued by my spasms, especially when I told them that nobody, even those in the medical field, knew why, how and to what extent they happened. I could also entertain them with amusing anecdotes that occurred as a result of my disability.

All this showed a combination of education, my acceptance of the disabilities, and the fact that I could find things occurring as a result of my spinal cord injury that I could laugh about. I hoped that students would be motivated by this, realising that it was possible to live and succeed despite difficult conditions and setbacks. After that, students were not distracted when I left to go to the toilet, or if I told them I couldn't move around the classroom since I had a bladder accident. One day I took a Year 10 class from the toilet at the back of the room after telling them that I had a serious bowel accident.

I also told them that the side effects of my dependence on drugs (pharmaceutical) was that it made me quite drowsy, sometimes to the extent that I would fall asleep on the bed in my bathroom during breaks. If I was late to class, they should check to see if I was asleep. Some of them weren't concerned enough to do that.

In this way I was able to assure them that I retained the credentials to teach, albeit from a wheelchair and that my part-time teaching would not impact badly on their education. My teaching from that time on differed little from what it had been before my accident. The main difference was my increased desire to achieve good results. To that end, I was overjoyed to teach two students, each of whom achieved the highest possible result in Maths B in Queensland. Several others achieved to the full extent of their ability. These successes were so important to me. The list of my disabilities was considerable; the list of my abilities needed to balance these out.

In my second year back at school, a number of other teachers moved into the staffroom. One in particular, Debbie Roche, was a welcome addition. I had previously shared a staffroom with her and had taught many similar maths classes. The other teachers in the staffroom were of considerable assistance, physically and emotionally.

During the four years of teaching after my accident, I took a much greater interest in the overall operation of the school. These were constructive criticisms made by a teacher who had taught at the school for thirty years. I think I wanted to show the staff that I wasn't just a passenger but that I cared about the School's performance, and was prepared to contribute positively. I started a Maths Problem-Solving Competition and the Kilometre Klub.

Often I would need help from other staff members and from students. Sometimes students would simply offer to push me up the hill or across the oval. While I could do this myself, and the exercise was useful, I always agreed, knowing the satisfaction that students got out of helping. One day, when I was out reassimilating myself with the school outside my limited domain, a couple of girls discretely suggested that I pull up my pants. If there is one frustrating dependency, it results from being unable to adjust your pants while confined to a wheelchair. I soon realised, as I did with other things, that you have to ask for help, however embarrassing it might at first seem.

Jana Morrisova was my case manager at school. She was very supportive and a trustworthy confidante. She had the ability to make necessary changes, be they administrative issues or physical aspects of my classroom. The principal, Wayne Troyahn, also showed great compassion. When I had an issue, I would write him a note and he would generally come down to discuss it. I found this hard to accept, that the school principal would put me ahead of all the other important matters he had to deal with. However, resolving these issues was very good for me, especially since my medical condition had delivered me hypertension. Ross Grimley and I did most of the Maths B teaching during this latter end of my career. He could be relied upon to help out with assessment or teaching problems. There were many other teachers with whom I interacted in a positive way. Without all their collective help, I think I may have ended my career sooner.

As a part of my Graduated Return to Work Program, meetings were held involving Jana, Wayne, Jan Arnold (from Regional Office), and me. At one stage I felt that certain people within the system expected much more than I was able to do. So, out of frustration, I prepared a memo for them as follows:

RETURN TO FULL TIME WORK WHAT IS NEEDED

1. *Ability to cope with tiredness.* Tiredness is due to movement around the classroom, early rising (5.30 am) in the morning to prepare for school, being in a wheelchair (my body aches and my legs spasm), and prescription drugs like valium and baclofen needed to reduce spasms, and stressful situations.
2. *Ability to cope with the general functions of a teacher.* These functions include access to the administration area, being able to use the

photocopier, being able to attend meetings after school, access around the school, and involvement in school activities.

3. *Ability to cope with depression.* I feel I have reached the stage when recovery (from paraplegia) is not going to happen.

One day, I was asked to supervise the class of an absent teacher. The teacher had left nothing for the class to do. I decided I would talk to them about people with disabilities. I emphasized that, although my disability was obvious, there were people with problems that weren't apparent, even to some of their best friends. This Year 9 class listened so intently that, even when the bell rang, nobody moved. After I let the class go, I sensed a couple of girls lingering. One approached me to tell me that she suffered severe depression as a result of a tragic family accident. She was so well-presented that I realised she was just the sort of person about whom I was talking. She thanked me for the talk and I offered to talk with her if ever she wanted to come to see me.

While I was still in the Spinal Unit, a poster on the wall beside the arm ergometer in the gym emphasised the importance of cardio-vascular exercise for people with spinal cord injuries. As I used the machine each day, I stared directly at the poster which suggested three options—an arm ergometer, such as the one I was using, pushing the wheelchair under some resistance, or swimming. I bought an arm ergometer which I used daily, (sometimes twice daily), but the terrain of our ten-acre property did not lend itself to regular wheelchair exercise, and I was never really a swimmer. One day, about two months after I was out of hospital, Cheryl Griggs rang to *tell* me that she would meet me at the Nambour pool at 1 pm the next day. Of course I did!

Cheryl is a wonderful person with endless compassion for people with disabilities. More than this, she involves herself selflessly with their rehabilitation. As well as starting me swimming, she insisted on me trying all measures of things to help with my physical situation. Cheryl did and still does this with many others. How huge a heart must this lady have?

She had a life-jacket for me to wear. The hoist was not in working order so I was helped down the steps in my shower chair. She tried a range of exercises to supplement some laps that I struggled through. Each week, I went to the pool. The hoist was soon fixed so that I didn't need to rely on others, (mostly strangers), to get me into or out of the pool. Another friend, Kathy Ashworth, (a qualified repatriation nurse), started to teach me how to swim with the assistance of a life-jacket. Each week I increased the number of laps until I reached 84, after which I concentrated on increasing my speed. It was a wonderful form of exercise that helped me both physically and mentally. It made the beer taste so much better that night.

One day I was swimming my laps when I looked down to see that I had no swimming togs on. I stopped immediately, holding onto the lane ropes. How long had I been like this? Had anyone seen me? My embarrassment was intense. I pulled myself down to the shallow end where I could rest on my knees and conceal my predicament. Where would my togs be? Would they float or sink? I eventually decided to pull myself along the lane rope to search for them. There they were, right down the deep end! If I just dive down—but I was wearing the life jacket and couldn't submerge sufficiently to get them! With all rationality gone, I thrashed around until at last I got them. Only then did I realise that it would be very difficult to put them on. The whole episode continued for some time until a light switched on in my head. Surely the other dozen people in the pool knew something was wrong! After all, from swimming laps to thrashing about in the pool was not what people do without something being wrong—even people in wheelchairs? So I swallowed my pride and called out, "Can somebody help me? I've lost my swimming togs!" All except one young boy were a good distance from me. He swam off as though he was in a race. An elderly man offered to help. Eventually I was clad again, and resumed my swimming.

This incident taught me a great lesson which I have passed on to many young people since. Little is to be gained by trying to hide your disabilities. People understand that there are some things you can't do and are only too willing to help. In so doing they don't think any less of you. In fact they tend to put themselves in your position and wonder how they would react. In balance, the whole incident resulted from the fact that I was prepared to place myself in a position where an embarrassing event could occur. I was swimming laps to help my recovery from, or assist my ability to cope with, a serious injury. So don't try to hide your disabilities, balance them out by displaying your abilities! It is also important to find such incidents amusing to the point where you are prepared to share them with others.

When I returned home from the Spinal Unit, I was determined to resume my cricket coaching. John was 12 and I had coached his team since they began cricket. At the start of the 2002/03 season, all the boys returned. While it was a little difficult coaching from a wheelchair, the boys and their parents were very co-operative at practice and at the games. It was frustrating not to be able to demonstrate things to them or to umpire their games, (from which I could learn more of their strengths and weaknesses), but Grant helped me with this. I didn't go softly on them as a result of this co-operation since I knew they had the capacity to work hard at the game, and the capabilities to excel. They improved to the point where we lost very narrowly in the final. I continued to coach them for the next two years when, in their last year of Junior Cricket, we won the final. There was much celebration, but the satisfaction I felt was immeasurable.

One day, when the boys had completed a session in which they did just about everything except what we had planned to do during practice that week, I sat all the boys on a seat in front of the Clubhouse. I told them in stern tones about the importance of fielding well and bowling to a plan. I had the undivided attention of all the players and many of their parents (who were not used to seeing me get upset). I told the boys to sit there and silently think over what I had told them. Then as I reversed my wheelchair, one of the tyres dropped through a grate covering a drain so that I toppled out of the chair. All I could see was the horrified and indecisive faces of the boys. Should they stay seated as they were told or jump up and help me back into the chair? As it was, many parents' hands helped me out. Perhaps God was punishing me for what I said to the boys!

I retired from teaching at the end of the 2006 school year. It was a very emotional time. I remembered the many times I had watched with envy, ceremonies celebrating other teachers' retirements. At those times, I thought the only difficult part would be making a speech. When it was my turn however, making the speech was easy until I began to thank and acknowledge Debbie. I had taught with Debbie throughout my thirty-one years at Nambour High School. We had taught similar classes virtually every year and helped each other out for that reason. We shared the same staffroom. I found Debbie a good listener when I was going through frustrating times, (which was often). Debbie was an outstanding teacher in every facet of the profession from the classroom to leadership and mentoring programs. So I relied often on her advice which was always given in a humble and compassionate way. I consider her to be the greatest positive influence and best friend I made during my teaching career.

I thought that retirement would give me more time to do less despite what other retirees had told me. Sleeping in was wonderful, especially if I happened to wake early and realized there was no reason not to go back to sleep. However, I had many commitments. One was to tutoring students, mainly in Maths. I had the pleasure of tutoring some real achievers like Allen Ledger. Most progressed well and their improvement provided me with much satisfaction. Another entry on the *Abilities* side of the ledger! I also continued my ties with the Nambour Cricket Club taking a management position with the seniors and generally helping out where I could.

The Rural Fire Services still brought their accounts to me for auditing. I did this, not only as a contribution to the local community, but because I thought it quite unjust for accountants to charge so much for small non-profit organizations.

Not enough people realize the satisfaction that is obtained by voluntary work or by taking on non-paying positions in various organizations. It gave me a sense of worth, and, while I don't expect a return, it will often occur in many different ways. I discovered this when I received so much help and support during and after my stay in the Spinal Unit.

Depression is inevitable! I just couldn't help thinking, from time to time, why me? It was a simple fall. A man admitted to the Spinal Unit shortly after me was the victim of a car accident in which he was not wearing a seatbelt, had just finished a long session at the pub and was a passenger in a vehicle which rolled. Yet he walked within weeks and was discharged! How did I deal with depression? I turned it into anger. I swore at my pot plants when I had a bladder accident. I punched the steering wheel when I had spasms. Then, when I realized how irrational that behaviour was, I snapped out of it. When I became rational again, I would enter all aspects of my life into a ledger in my mind. On one side were my disabilities; on the other were my abilities. Like accountants, I was satisfied only when I could at least balance the ledger. To do this I tried to increase my abilities. One of these was teaching. Others included cricket coaching, tutoring, guest speaking, auditing books, swimming, gardening and even attending meetings, functions or parties. I reached the stage where I couldn't do much more to reduce my disabilities. That possibility was in the hands of scientists conducting stem cell research and other possible remedies for people with spinal cord injuries.

I kept up the tutoring. While it was taxing, especially as programs of work changed in the senior school, I felt as though I was contributing to the students' progress. I was also using my motivational skills. Some began in Year 9 and continued through to Year 12. Others arrived only after reaching Year 11 or 12 when maths becomes quite challenging. Some students were high achievers in other subjects, but were determined to at least pass Maths B and not take the easy option of dropping back to Maths A. It was a pleasure to harness their resolve. Others were very good at Maths but wanted to become even better or at least maintain their high level.

An intriguing but surprising ability that I attained was that of public speaking. Whether it was because I captured the attention of the audience more easily because I was sitting in a wheelchair, or perhaps I sensed no reason to be nervous about finding the appropriate words or constructing suitable sentences. I did not do it for public recognition, (although I knew it would have a motivational influence on some people in the audience), but to help balance the ledger. Whatever, I know I felt much better afterwards. I approached the Spinal Education Awareness Team (SEAT) to offer my services to visit local schools and talk to students about spinal injuries. Each time I knew there were questions students wanted to ask but didn't, questions like, "*How do you use the toilet?*" or, "*Why are your feet tied to the footplate?*" So I framed part of my talk around some of these unspoken questions.

Before I retired from teaching, I had the desire to write a book. My life had taken a severe turn for the worst leading me in an unplanned and unwanted direction. I wanted to share this experience with others, even strangers. I also wanted the thrill of achieving something I wouldn't otherwise have attempted—balancing that ledger again. There were times when I found it easy to relate stories, but there were long periods of time when I could not get motivated to write. I would read what I had already written and each time it seemed less convincing. The anecdotes that were supposed to capture the readers' imagination or amuse them increasingly seemed bland.

When Dad died in May, 2007, I found a black box in his study. He made me aware of its existence prior to his death. It contained a book detailing my parents' financial records. I also knew it contained copies of their wills. The rest of its contents were a pleasant although touching surprise. One letter contained every detail of Dad's planned funeral and graveside service. Since Dad was a devout Christian and an elder in the Presbyterian Church, the minister was not surprised at the existence of this letter. I also found a letter addressed, "To Lindsay Turnbull on the Death of his Father, Keith Richard Turnbull". *It was quite a moving experience to open this letter, which I did in private. The box also contained much of Dad's writings—* "My Memoirs of Teaching", "The Autobiography of Keith Richard Turnbull", *(of which we found only 5 pages), many copies of skits that Dad had performed at the annual church concert, diaries of trips he and Mum had taken and special letters he had received from relatives and friends.*

At his funeral, I delivered the following eulogy which I think sums up his life.

"Dad had many faces, the collection of which made him the great man he was.

*Dad had a **stern face**, a face he needed to raise his children. A face he needed when, as Jill recalled, she would approach Dad with,* "It's alright by Mum, if it's alright by you, that I can go to Lisa's party on Saturday night". "Well it's not alright by me!" "But Sharon and Lynelle are going!!" "I don't care if the Queen's Mother is going, you're not. I know what happens at these parties." *He also needed a stern face because he was our teacher, in my case, for all but one term of my years at Primary School.*

*Dad also had a **humorous face**. He found humour in many things, even in his pastoral care activities. I remember one incident which occurred on one of our many family holidays. We had gone to a fairly remote place when after a short time disaster struck—the handle on the teapot broke. While despair was evident on the faces of all, I told them I had some Super Glue, glue that, with only one drop, will hold anything together. So I applied the glue, (two drops to be sure), held the broken parts together for 10 minutes, (to be sure), and then let go. As I removed my hand the teapot moved with it. Dad laughed so much the tears rolled down his face and his whole body convulsed in unison.*

*Dad had a **competitive face**. In all the sport I played with him it was quite evident that winning was almost the only thing that brought out the enjoyment in sport. When I played sport against him—table tennis or tennis, he would use every tactic to put me off my game so that I would become furiously over-ambitious resulting in his inevitable win. But his competitiveness also extended to games like scrabble. We knew that he would go to his grave convinced that Mum got a disproportionate number of "s's" and blanks.*

*But Dad also had a **compassionate face**. Often, while the family was enjoying each other's company, Dad would get dressed up and set off for the hospital with a list of people he was to visit. Many times, he would return home disclosing that most were not there. Still his demeanour was serene. When he helped people with their shopping or to take them places, (especially Arthur), he always had something interesting or amusing to say which indicated that he didn't find it to be an imposition.*

Finally, Dad left me a letter which finished with the words, "His life shall never end, for Jesus is his Saviour and Friend"."

As I read and reread Dad's literary works, it struck me how important it was for the elderly to document their lives, or at least aspects of it, for the benefit and interest of future generations. Of course, I am not elderly, but I have something to tell. In a world in which nearly everything is changing rapidly, the lives of people in past generations is of great interest, especially to their young descendants.

When Dad was in Junior (Year 10) at Brisbane State High School, he and his classmates were invited to complete a short course of ten weeks in teaching before being posted to fill the vacancies created by the many teachers who enlisted for the Second World War. Although he wanted to be a journalist, Dad accepted. On completion of the course, Dad was appointed to Rocky Point (north of Mossman). The youngest in a family of eight, he was put on the train by his mother at the tender age of seventeen, en route to this most northerly destination, a school *in a war zone.* He was met in Cairns by friends of the family, who organised a ride for him on an American troop carrier. However, they encountered floods and at one stage Dad tried unsuccessfully to swim a flooded river and had to be rescued by the mailman. When he at last took up duty, he found the school, perched on a cliff overlooking the ocean to be quite attractive. However, the Battle of the Coral Sea was happening and at one stage he and his pupils had to rescue airmen who made a forced landing on the beach nearby. Dad moved to many areas around the State. When at a one-teacher school at Pentland, he was asked to conduct a funeral service for a local. Apparently, no one else was available to do it. It was in school time. I think Mum sat in front of the classes while he was away. It was not possible to get supply teachers out there.

Mum, on the other hand, told us little of her life. I knew it was the life of a country girl whose parents were farm labourers. However, riding a horse to school, entertaining one another with family sing-alongs, moving from farm to farm and living such a frugal existence were all of great interest to me.

Mum has the "Wisdom of Solomon". During my upbringing, Mum and Dad complemented each other very well as parents. However, it was Mum to whom I turned whenever I needed something. Mum taught me to drive. She would send me parcels and letters while I was at university that usually contained a small amount of money and a fruit cake. She had subtle ways of leading me towards the right course of action.

Days, weeks and months went by when I couldn't motivate myself to write. I did some gardening, watched TV and didn't go out much. Sometimes I didn't even go downstairs. I completed my stretches and arm-cycling, but after finishing, I felt that they had done nothing for me. It seemed like the start of another depressing day. It was raining so I should have been happy being on a small acreage and relying on tank water. The Great Flood would struggle to reach our home on the hill. My bottom ached—not because I was using the BMX wheels while my other wheels were being fixed, or that I had forgotten to do pressure lifts. My eyes felt sore as though I had been in the sun all day. The computer had broken down and it looked as though the technician wasn't going to arrive. He did, but the news wasn't good!

The wet weather had been with us almost non-stop since the New Year. Our cricket teams had a serious talk, but so many of our practice sessions and match days were washed out taking all the resolve with it.

No painting occurred again today. No more cleaning of the dining room which made it and its contents still inaccessible to me. The window cleaning job which John was supposed to do had ceased less than a quarter of the way through. There was just so much of the house that needed work or cleaning done. I wish I had a licence to throw out anything that we didn't need! All Greg's belongings were still where he left them, under the house, before going to Canada. There was no cricket on TV that day. The press was full of commentary from uninformed sources about how unsportsmanlike were the Australian cricketers. And these comments came from Australian as well as overseas sportspeople. They had another thing in common, I believe—they all envied the success of the Australian cricketers. I hope they have overwhelming victories over all their opponents.

Tennis dominates TV. Again everyone talks up Lleyton Hewitt. When will they learn? He has been such a great player but Australians place so much pressure on him, then, when he loses, they are all so critical. Tennis players are highly overpaid and the same players win all the tournaments. I don't like individual sports!

This is summer, the holidays, when people go to the beach. I can't get down on the beach, let alone swim. I used to be able to do it, but didn't. Now I would like to but can't. Why didn't I take the family overseas on a holiday when I could? Why didn't I spend more time with them on activities that I now can't do? So many things were waiting for my retirement. Now look at me—overweight, always depending on people for help, swallowing tablets that only slow my regression, and getting my greatest thrills out of completing crosswords and sudoku puzzles.

Today I have had one bladder accident so far, and no one else was home. Yesterday I had three, and nobody can tell me why it happens!

Do people really know what it is like to suffer paraplegia? Even if I told them, would they understand what it is like to be incontinent? To know that at any time, my bladder or bowels would cause me great embarrassment and inconvenience? That I have lost my sexual functions? That I have less than half of my lung capacity? That I can go only where my wheelchair will go? That I can't reach things? That anything left on the floor will probably be in the way?

Good fortune soon changes one's outlook!

Retirement gave Liz and me the opportunity to travel. We flew to Melbourne to see Fiona and Jim, and drove to Sydney to see Bronwyn and other relatives. One year we undertook a four-week holiday, driving to Adelaide down the western route through New South Wales crossing the border at Balranald into Victoria. We detoured so as to see Manangatang, a small Victorian town where Liz lived as a child. At Adelaide we stayed with cousin Peter and Jenny. They showed us around Adelaide and interesting parts of the State like the old mining town of Burra. A trip to South Australia is incomplete without visiting some famous wine-making districts. Peter and Jenny were very good to us. We drove to Mornington after leaving Adelaide. The trip included the Great Ocean Road, a spectacular drive made even more so when the weather is bad.

Trips like these increased my confidence in travelling, living in alternative accommodation, and generally improvising. Before long, we were starting to talk of an overseas trip. In June of 2009, we flew out of Brisbane on a flight to London via Bangkok.

Long before I retired, I had expressed a wish to visit the United Kingdom and Ireland on a sight-seeing holiday that coincided with an Ashes tour (Australia v's England in cricket in England and Wales). Planning started with a visit to a travel agency. However, as I should have expected, there were many problems e.g. no coach tours throughout Europe were wheelchair-accessible. So we began to make bookings and other arrangements on the internet. We booked hotel accommodation, train trips, hire cars, flights and entry to special events.

Ashes Test matches are still the highlight on the cricket calendar for the original combatants of the sport. I have attended many such tests in Australia, mainly Brisbane, and they always attract big attendances.

The problem would be getting tickets for the Tests in England and Wales, given that their ground capacities are much smaller than those in Australia. In the end I was able to obtain tickets for each Test, although not for every day. I think I would have been unable to attend every day because of my physical limitations. I also had to remember that we had so many places apart from the cricket grounds that we wanted to see.

To this day, I think the best thing I did was to keep a diary of each day's activities, even if it meant staying up quite late at night.

TOUR OF THE U.K. AND IRELAND
(AND PARIS FOR A DAY)

22/06/2009

It was a very early start—stretches at 5.00am. There was time for some breakfast since we were ahead of schedule, or so we thought. The planned 8.00am departure happened 45 minutes late. We drove to Brisbane in heavy rain which eased as we approached the airport. We had plenty of time at the domestic terminal with Greg. We boarded a Qantas flight to Sydney. Then the panic set in as we arrived there. How would we get to the international airport, then through customs and be first to board, as is the practice for passengers in wheelchairs? However, we were taken by a steward through a labyrinth which I could never have negotiated alone. I was asked if I would like to use the toilet which I did only to hear my name called over the public address whilst in there. As a result, we were last to board. BA10 departed on time at 4.45pm for Bangkok. Complimentary drinks—relax!

I think it is impossible to relax for any extended period of time. The physical options in an aeroplane seat are few. The TV screen meant to entertain, starts to become a tonic. Lights out—no reading, crosswords, sudokus, etc—try to sleep. Watching our progress on the screen was like watching grass grow. But it wasn't all bad—the stewards constantly served drinks and food.

23/06/2009

The stopover at Bangkok was for refuelling. We were told that we would all need to disembark, taking our hand luggage with us. I explained to one of the stewards that my wheelchair was in cargo. After consultation with someone, she came back to say that Liz and I could remain on the plane. I explained, however, that I needed to use the toilet. When we landed and all other passengers had left the plane, stewards brought me the aisle chair that was kept on the plane. I transferred into it after which they wheeled me to the plane's toilet. It was completely inaccessible to me. So they decided I should go to the toilet in the airport. I was transferred on the boarding ramp into an airport wheelchair. Two airport employees wheeled me, in a very casual manner, to the nearest toilet. With Liz's help, but still great difficulty, I transferred onto the toilet seat. Using the toilet is not easy for people with spinal cord injuries and usually requires the use of a shower chair/commode, which I didn't have. However, with time running out, my patience evaporated quickly. When the announcement came over the public address calling for Mr and Mrs Turnbull to board their plane, anxiety turned to panic. All this time, the two airport stewards showed little concern. Eventually, my toileting was finished and we emerged to be wheeled by these two men at a leisurely pace back to the boarding ramp. I avoided looking at any of the other passengers so as not to see their frustration at being kept waiting. Only when I was back in my seat did my blood pressure begin to ease. During this whole episode, it never registered with me that, for the first time, I had ventured into foreign territory, albeit only an airport!

At some stage during the flight, the date changed. Then some daylight, although the cabin crew insisted that all windows be kept closed as some passengers were still sleeping. We touched down in London—has this really happened?

Andy and Will were there to greet us. Getting through customs was very quick; I suspect because I was in a wheelchair and getting personal attention. Andy had organised for us to have a shower there. It's as well I did since I had suffered a bowel accident after one of the wheelchair transfers. I was able to put on some clean clothes, had a cup of coffee and followed Andy to the car. While all this seemed so easy, I could not have done it unassisted.

The drive to East Chinnok was mostly along a motorway where the only speed limit was the capacity of the car's motor. Not long after leaving London and entering the countryside, the drive became very enjoyable. So green! All the houses seem to be built in the hollows, whereas back in Queensland, they are built on the hills (I suppose to get the breeze, a view and to avoid the floods). Soon, we passed Stonehenge, hardly the tourist attraction I had expected to see. We arrived at Andrew and Chris's place to find a real English stone cottage with a colourful garden where we enjoyed lunch in the sunshine. In fact, it was still sunshine much later—we weren't still having lunch but had progressed to dinner. Although we were both tired, we waited up as long as we could to avoid the effects of jetlag.

During the afternoon, Andy and I went for a push through the township. All houses are very old—16th to 18th centuries. A few were heritage-listed, but not necessarily maintained to that standard. The footpaths are very narrow as is the main road through the town. We had to take our chances when crossing the road but, in so doing, the right front castor collapsed when I hit the curb. Andy pushed me home as I balanced on the three good wheels. A phone call extracted a promise to repair the chair in a nearby town.

24/06/09

After breakfast, we headed off to Martoc. What a drive! Despite there being quite a lot of traffic, the roads were narrow with no verge at all. In fact, the hedges reached the edge of the road so that passing required good manners, patience, being prepared to stop or even reverse to a gap in the hedge. Then when crossing a hill, a magnificent view of the countryside would briefly appear before being hidden by the hedge once again. Small villages with shopfronts extending to the side of the road, stately churches, manors, converted stables or workers' cottages made the towns the quaint places I had imagined but never seen—vastly different to Australia. I suppose it is one of the reasons for this trip.

Where to park? Just here will do! People here park in any lane, facing in either direction. Chances are there are more cars/trucks in front of them, and a line of traffic behind them. Eventually you take your chances, swing out into the other lane and hope that the on-coming traffic will let you through. The next best option is a stalemate.

We arrived at a shop that seemed to cater for many things, including, I hoped, the parts and tools needed to repair my wheelchair. The owner assured Liz he could fix the wheelchair. He spoke to Liz and Chris about what needed to be done, but ignored me. (This was not the first time this has happened but I will never get used to it. I get the feeling that, perhaps innocently, some people believe my physical disability effects my mental capacity as well.) The shop lent me a wheelchair, the only similarity being that it had 4 wheels, none of which could be self-propelled.

25/06/2009

Eventually we received the call and returned to pick up the wheelchair. Perhaps it was my accent; perhaps because I was in a wheelchair, but that wheelchair repairer took me for a ride (not literally—financially). They had sent to London to get a full set of castors and supports for the front (when only a new wheel was required). Then there was all the labour. At least I now have one spare wheel!

We picked up Andy from golf. While waiting I felt the need for a pint of Carlsberg. I met his golf partners over a drink. Another English idiosyncrasy—they shared a pot of tea (on a warm summer's day).

To finish off the day, I had a severe bowel accident. After an hour, the chair, bed and I were cleaned up, thanks to Liz. (No point in leaving out all the lowlights as well as the highlights in this diary).

26/6/09

I was so tired, I slept through a storm, (apparently including thunder and lightning). Still, I was up early for our big day. We piled into Chris' car and set off for Bishops Lyndeard, near Taunton (of Ian Botham and Viv Richards fame when the Somerset Cricket Club was much stronger). Here we boarded a steam train, driven and fully staffed by volunteers splendidly dressed in traditional railway uniforms of The West Somerset Railway, the oldest commercial railway in the UK. So enthusiastic are these people that they not only give up their time but they also pay for their uniforms. I rode in the guard van, not for disciplinary reasons, but to accommodate the wheelchair. The train travels west-north-west until it reaches the Bristol Channel. We disembarked at Dunster, pushed/walked up to the village which was crowded with tourists, then proceeded up the steep hill to Dunster Castle. Having worn out both arms and all three pushers, we were pleased to hear at the entrance that a courtesy bus would drive us up the remainder of the hill. The castle was not accessible but the Tennants' Hall was. It contained a history of the castle. In 1376 it was bought by the Lutterills for £1332. Eventually it was passed over to the National Trust. The Lutterills were ancestors of Liz and Andy on the de Bomford side which heightened their interest. We lunched at the Tea Rooms. I ordered sandwiches which they called doorstop sandwiches. It was basically two loaves of bread held together by butter, ham and salad (and possibly araldite). I couldn't finish the second half so a strong waiter with block and tackle cleared it away. Well fed, we headed back to the train and had an interesting trip home. The early morning rain and low cloud had given way to a reasonably clear day.

27/6/09

I had an enforced sleep-in to treat an infected toe and a pressure sore on my bottom (probably the result of too many awkward transfers on the trip over). I sat on my cushion for the Sydney to Bangkok leg, but found it too difficult so stowed the cushion in the overhead lockers for the second leg of the flight to London.

That evening we attended the East Chinnok Annual Barn Dance organised by the local provincial council (they also organise Guy Falkes Night and a Christmas party). £5 entry included a BBQ (which Andy cooked). Locals of all ages attended. I tried the local cider donated by a farmer, but opted for the local bitter ale, called Piddle. Four pints of Piddle and I had to look for a secluded place.

28/6/09

Another quiet day! We visited Neville and Margaret next door for morning tea and a view of their colourful English garden, complete with a small stream flowing through it. Chris was off on a charity walk at a local castle. Andy was cleaning up after the Barn Dance.

We had an easy afternoon when I wrote my emails, some postcards and booked an extra night in London. A savoury, enticing smell was coming from the kitchen—roast chicken and vegies! I am looking forward to that and to tomorrow.

29/6/09

We left East Chinnok at about 1pm. Andy drove us to Bristol airport, carefully dodging the huge traffic still exiting Glastonbury, a big music festival. We were looked after very well. Bristol Airport does not have any boarding chutes, so we were put on a bus and taken to the plane on the tarmac. I was loaded on to a lift, transferred into an aisle chair and moved across to the window seat. The plane flew north over the Bristol Channel with the spectacular bridges below us, *west across southern Wales along the edge of the Channel and then over the Irish Sea (where I could see all the ferries). Shortly afterwards I caught my first sight of Ireland and yes, it was very green!*

The view of the countryside of Ireland, (and most of the UK), is quite different to that of Australia. From the air, it looked like a jigsaw picture of farms with small paddocks separated by hedges, and often not rectangular. We could see Waterford and Rosslaire, where most ferries dock. After an hour-long flight, we landed in Cork. From here, we were starting to struggle with communication. I was looked after by a steward who led me through the small airport to collect our luggage and then to the Hertz counter to collect our hire car, a Toyota Corolla. What happened to customs? With a minimum of trouble, we drove to our hotel, Ashlee Lodge in Tower, Blarney. After checking in, (it was already 7.30pm), we went for a push. Not far down a hill was a pub, the Huntsman, where we had a few drinks—me, two pints of Murphies, and Liz, an Irish version of lemon, lime and bitters. We were served toasted sandwiches even though it was 9pm. A steep push home and back to our excellent accessible room.

30/6/09

What a day! The way to start a big day of sightseeing in Ireland is to have a full Irish breakfast—not in the hotel, not on the main road, but in a back street in Macroon, as we did. Out comes a pot of tea, then a full plate containing 3 bacon rashers, an egg, 3 sausages, 2 white puddings, 2 potato patties and 2 slices of toast. Then, because it won't fit on the plate, out comes a bowl of baked beans and a bowl of mushrooms. If that wasn't enough, out came more slices of freshly baked bread with jams, honey etc. AND she asked if we wanted more! This means you have more time for sightseeing, since you don't need morning tea, lunch, or afternoon tea.

Relieved of our hunger pains, we embarked on a drive around the Ring of Kerry. To describe it and to photograph it does not do it justice! Everyone needs to experience it. The lakes, the steep and craggy hills, the waterfalls, rushing streams, sheep, cattle, and peat farms, and then we arrived at the Atlantic coast. I had now seen the three great oceans!

Finally, leaving the Ring we headed north to Tralee and on to . . .
A middle-aged man and his wife
Were having the trip of their life,
Shunning cream and strawberry
They drove the Ring of Kerry
But then they ran into strife.
(They got lost!!)
I thought I had the directions to our hotel in Limerick included in the folder with the booking invoice. I couldn't find the directions so we couldn't find the hotel until, by good fortune, we found it on the outskirts of town. With darkness

delayed in this part of the world, we seemed to arrive late, eat late and struggle to get up in the morning and stay awake during the day. Tomorrow will be a shorter drive.

1/7/09

*Again we left our hotel quite late at about 10am. It seems to take us about three hours to get ready to leave half an hour for my stretching, one to one and a half hours for me in the bathroom (depending on its accessibility), half an hour for breakfast, half an hour to pack up the shower chair and then the car. If only I could hurry Liz up a bit! It was **not** to be a short drive.*

The hotel was good, not as good as Ashlee Lodge in Blarney, but also wheelchair-friendly. We stopped after a few kilometres at Bunratty Castle, but since little of it was accessible, we didn't go inside.

We drove on through Ennis to the Cliffs of Moher, a spectacular part of the west coast with sheer cliffs and long walking trails. I was unable to push very far, but Liz climbed the stairs to the top where there was a fortress. In the distance, (not particularly far since it was raining), I could see another. Rain here takes some time to get you wet, but it can be persistent.

We followed the coastline to Galway which is quite a large town overlooking the famous Galway Bay (not, as I was to discover, the home of Galway Pipe port). We did not stop since it was getting quite late. Passing many loughs enclosed by hilly countryside we came across Coonemara NP on our way to Clifden on the coast. We thought the trip to here was slow, but from here to Westport was even slower. The 100km/h signs were meaningless since we averaged about 70 km/h. All the time, however, the scenery was spectacular—water, mountains and small villages. We arrived at our B & B to be greeted by very hospitable hosts. The bedroom and bathroom were both accessible and immaculate with nothing neglected. The small wrapped item left on the towels turned out to be chocolate, (otherwise it was the best soap I have ever eaten). We had cheese and biscuits and some fruit for tea, then bed!

2/7/09

Today started out well with a breakfast that outdid anything we have had. Leaving the Garden Gates, we set off for Derry (the name most people use for Londonderry). Mindful of the late arrivals on the previous three nights, we restricted our stops. We planned to have plenty of time to see Donegal Castle overlooking the picturesque Donegal Bay. Signage in Ireland can be difficult to read, especially when it is written in English and Gaelic, with Gaelic usually on top. They tend to place the sign at the point where you turn, with little or no prior warning. Consequently, when you get to an intersection, you need to speed-read a short story before turning (and hope you are in the correct lane). Speaking of lanes, in Ireland there is generally just one lane (to accommodate traffic in both directions) which is quite wide. For two small cars it can become two lanes. With one small and one large vehicle, or two large vehicles it becomes an argument.

The end result was that we saw the Bay but not the Castle. So we decided to get to Derry ASAP in time to have a tour of the city. Just before Derry, we were advised that we were in Northern Ireland and speed limits were shown in miles per hour.

We found our hotel without too much trouble. However, the only parking was in a parking station nearby. We unpacked and used a shopping trolley to carry our belongings. Later we set off for a push down towards the old walled city. Parts of the wall still exist. Some of the original buildings could also be seen, but generally the place was in a state of disrepair. Sad really because it has a remarkable history!

3/7/09

Again a late start from Derry! We took the detour to the north coast where we stopped at the Giant's Causeway. This amazing geological, or to the locals wishing to drum up business, legendary, place is heritage-listed. After a quick look through the souvenir shop, we rode on a bus to the most accessible part at which we took many photos. The Causeway is linked to Scotland where there is an identical structure. Basalt rock cooling quickly during the ice-age cracked in columns, mostly hexagonal, that creates a tessellation incorporating the columns.

It was then an easy drive to Belfast. Belfast is not the dangerous sectarian place that it once was. When we found our hotel, we thought we had enjoyed a good day. We were allocated Room 304. It had an inaccessible bathroom. I went to the reception desk for an explanation. I calmly produced my reservation confirmation dated May 19th. After some time and many apologies, we were offered another room, 104, accessible but with two single beds which was quite acceptable. As a token of their regret, we were offered free breakfasts. I accepted, and then we went for a push around the city. When we returned, we had a drink in the bar. The manager approached us there to say that, regretfully, Room 104 was booked to someone else. He could see I was about to explode, so he quickly offered to book us into another hotel at their expense. He ordered the bar attendant to supply us with free drinks in the meantime. We accepted the drinks but declined the offer of another hotel. He departed, after offering us free dinners, and returned to say that his porters would relocate our belongings to Room 404. He agreed to refund our payment in full. Although our room was not accessible, we had at least got some recompense (and it certainly wasn't the first time we had found ourselves in an unsuitable room). It pays to stand up, or in my case sit down, with an uncompromising demeanour, insisting on your rights. I went back to our room reflecting that, although it was inaccessible, we had free accommodation, drinks, dinner and breakfast. So I completed my diary and prepared for bed. **But there was no water!!** *Liz went down to reception to find an even more frazzled manager* *since there was no water throughout the hotel. He gave her a glass of water with which we could clean our teeth and for me to take my tablets. What a day!! Time for bed!*

The hotel is the Jury's Inn. I recommend it!

4/7/09

To the manager's credit, he was there at breakfast this morning, helping to serve and clean. After yesterday's problems he had every reason to be on special leave. We had a substantial, (and nourishing, Fiona), breakfast and set off for Dublin, looking forward to re-entering the Republic. We arrived early enough there to park in the city and push around the shops, information centres and through Trinity College. The courtyard and paths were cobblestone—very effective, obviously historic but awkward in a wheelchair. We have brochures and maps to study tonight to compile a program for tomorrow.

5/7/09

For our second day in Dublin, we drove into the tourist area, being a Sunday, with every intention of taking a sight-seeing tour of the city in a bus. We passed the Guinness Storehouse and, knowing the bus stopped there, parked and went in to take a tour. There were 9 floors, each tracing the process of producing the beer and the history of the development of the product as a universal drink. On one floor was a tasting bar. How many tastes are there in a pint? On the top floor is a bar, fully enclosed by glass, providing not only a panoramic view of the city, but also another free beer (or two if your wife doesn't like Guinness).

After more than two hours in there (the building, not the bar), we drove on to look at different sites rather than take the bus. We stopped to eat on the way back to the hotel for an early night.

6/7/09

We decided that we must have a GPS navigator. So we drove to the local shopping centre. There was one for a bargain price containing 2009 maps for all countries at, guess where? Hervey Norman!! We set it up and drove off to Waterford. On the way we saw a sign indicating the turn-off to The Curragh, a famous racetrack. Compared to racetracks in Australia it is huge, perhaps because they have hurdling and steeple-chasing there.

A little further on we came upon the Irish National Stud, which combined with a Japanese Garden as a tourist attraction. The guided tour of the stud farm was the highlight. Eight stallions are stabled there. Each has its own stable and paddock. They stay in the paddock from 9am to 5pm unless they have a job to do. Each covers about 150 mares each season. One of these, Invincible Spirit, has served as many as 194 in a season. A champion sprinter himself, he holds the world record for the number of 2 year-old winners in a season. €60 000 will buy your mare a service from him. Some are "shuttle stallions" and one was being loaded to go to Australia while we were there.

One gelding is also kept there—Vintage Crop of Melbourne Cup fame. He has his own stable and paddock. I pushed through the rain and mud with Liz to see Invincible Spirit and Vintage Crop in their paddocks. They came up to us and posed for photos.

This was our 7th day in Ireland. It has rained every day. In fact, across "the pond" in Wales, rain is threatening the First Test in Cardiff. Tomorrow, we drive back to Dublin, return the car and catch a late flight to Cardiff.

7/7/09

We left Waterford, after Liz had a tour through the Waterford Crystal Centre, and headed back to Dublin. The trip again emphasised the difficulties/frustrations of driving in Ireland. The main road between these two large cities frequently passes directly through small crowded villages. It has lots of roundabouts, some with traffic lights, no passing lanes and, despite showing a speed limit of 100 km/h, it was a winding road where speeds of only 60 to 80 km/h are possible. Fortunately, we allowed for this having been pre-warned by locals.

We returned the car and spent a couple of hours in the airport waiting for our flight to Cardiff. We had some problems with the baggage being over-weight according to an over-zealous attendant, but that was sorted.

The above was written while we were waiting at the airport. I should have known better—we were travelling Irish Airlines.

Having checked in very early and informed the receptionist, as we always do, that since I can't walk, I would need assistance to transfer to an aisle chair at the boarding gate. Nobody arrived and the passengers were boarding. Many conversations via telephone still failed to produce results. I was taken down the lift and onto the tarmac waiting by the plane as the passengers and flight crew looked down at me. And I waited! Eventually someone turned up but without the chair. Then when it arrived, I was taken up the stairs and lifted into my seat. So why was I waiting for a chair?

The plane arrived in Cardiff 20 minutes late.

8/7/09

The First Day of the First Test! Grant, Betty, Allen and Maryanne were booked into the same hotel—the Big Sleep, in the centre of the city. After breakfast, Grant and I set off for the cricket, a short push/walk from the hotel. We arrived early. The Glamorgan Cricket Club had organised a large team of helpers. We were met outside the grounds and escorted to our positions. Whenever I went anywhere, there was a team of helpers to escort me to the toilet or food vans. Sophia Gardens is a small ground by Australian standards, with a seating capacity of just over 16 thousand. Despite it being advertised as a sell-out, there were many vacant seats. This was probably due to the tickets held by the scalpers outside. While the friendliness and helpfulness of the officials was superb, facilities could not cater for the crowd. The line-up at the toilets was always at least 30 men, the food stalls were difficult to access, and people waited in a large queue for drinks.

Since Grant and I had attended the First Day of the First Test in Australia for a long time, we decided to celebrate this one with a pint. But the bars didn't open until starting time, 11am!

The love of singing by the Welsh was one of the features of the day's entertainment. Not only the singing of the anthems, the Welsh first and the British last (which upset the English officials), but also the lunch and tea-time intervals when Sean Ruane, aided by a Welsh chorus, sang many traditional Welsh songs. The crowd joined in. I don't think that would work in Australia!

This was the first test ever played in Wales even though the local Glamorgan Cricket Club has a long history of participation in County Cricket and has supplied many players to the England team.

England won the toss and had no hesitation in batting. Johnson and Hilfenhaus, a surprise selection, opened the bowling with both getting little assistance through the air or off the wicket. But all the Australian bowlers worked hard and the Englishmen mostly got good starts but gave up their wickets with poor shots. Three wickets in the first session but none in the second saw England starting to build up a big score.

Grant helped me back to the city after stumps and we met the others there for dinner.

9/7/09

Liz and I had a leisurely walk/push to the cricket ground for Day 2 of the First Test after breakfast and bidding farewell to the Ledgers. Along the pathway to the ground was a sign, "The Old South Wales welcomes the New South Wales". You see, the Australian selectors are not the only ones who think the game is played in only one State in Australia!

We met Kobi Griggs at the ground. He was able to sit beside us. We enjoyed watching Australia build up a big score after England had improved their overnight score to 435. By stumps, both Kattich and Ponting had reached their centuries. The only time England seemed to have any penetration was when Flintoff bowled. He soon worked out Hughes's weakness, playing recklessly to shortish deliveries outside off-stump.

10/7/09

Today started very early with a visit from a doctor. I had developed pressure sores on both heels and my left big toe. They were also infected. He called for an ambulance which took me to Bandoch Hospital. All staff were very friendly and capable. I seemed to receive special attention—because I was paraplegic? Because I was Australian? Or because I had an unusual injury? I couldn't help thinking of the trouble I had gone to in order to get tickets for today. And how was Ross getting on at the ground by himself—would I be discharged in time to get there to see some cricket? Later when it was time for play to start, I asked a nurse if the cricket was being telecast. Her reaction and those of the other hospital staff made me realise that the Welsh were not great fans of the sport. One nurse, Sarah, said that her father would be following the game. She rang him from time to time and passed the news on to me that, "Players called North and Heading were doing very well and Australia was winning comfortably". I was very appreciative of the trouble she went to although the news made me more impatient to get to the ground. Doctors, radiologists, chiropodists and a "wound nurse" attended me from time to time. They scraped out the infected parts, dressed the sores, injected me with antibiotics then, with Sarah's urging, signed me out. Sarah hurried pharmacy who gave me a suitcase full of penicillin. She had a taxi waiting and after thanking her with great sincerity, I headed off for the cricket ground. I entered to see the covers on the pitch. I rang Ross only to find that he had left when it started to rain. More rain fell! Then as soon as it stopped, the covers were removed and play soon resumed. There was plenty of daylight to make up for lost time. I couldn't stay for long since we were catching the train that evening to Bristol. I also realised that I would have to push back to the railway station unassisted. I met Liz there. She had carried the entire luggage, including the shower chair to the station. We were assisted onto the train and departed for Bristol.

Our hotel in Bristol was across from the railway station. The porter kindly allowed us to take the baggage trolley to the hotel. The hotel was quite inaccessible—my shower chair would not go over the toilet or into the shower. Liz had to rearrange the single beds so that I could access one. We were too tired to complain. We went to bed without eating.

11/7/09

With tremendous difficulty, especially for Liz, we left the hotel loaded up with our baggage and headed for the railway station. We got a train to Yeovil where Andrew met us and took us to East Chinnok. Later that morning, we all drove to the Yeovilton Air (Navy) Base where there was an air display. Unfortunately, the weather, rain and low cloud, prevented some of the flying, especially the Vulcan, one of the highlights of the show. A range of helicopters, however, put on an impressive display. Nevertheless, the hospitality of Andrew and Chris's friends provided us with a very nice lunch and a generous supply of drinks. We enjoyed dinner at a local pub that evening.

I saw no cricket today but the intermittent scores told me that Australia had pushed on and on with Clarke, North and Haddin backing up Ponting and Kattich at the crease. A record four centuries—Kattich, Ponting, North and Haddin—plus an 81 from Clarke meant that the only hope for England was to save the game. A timely declaration at 6/674 enabled Australia to pick up two late wickets. Perhaps it was the nature of the people there but very few seemed interested in the cricket. Some said it would obviously be a draw.

12/7/09
After a quiet morning during which I slept in, then completed my morning rituals, I sat down to watch some cricket **on TV.** *Meanwhile Liz and Andy had gone out to make some important purchases, one of which was a cheap mobile phone. We had discovered, the expensive way, that being on International Roaming meant that if Grant called me, he paid for the call to go back to Australia, then to my provider in Australia, and finally from there to my mobile in the UK, (for which I paid). The long and short of it all was that when we communicated with each other, we both incurred a considerable charge.*

After lunch, Andy drove me to the Yeovil Hospital where I waited in Casualty, with no cricket on a TV, before being seen by a doctor. She had to inspect and then authorise the redressing of my sores. I arrived home just in time to see the gripping finale to the Test—one that got away from us.

After another delicious meal prepared by Andy and Chris, (both keen and able cooks), I put my injuries to bed, having gone so far as to decline a second port.

13/7/09
We rose early, said goodbye to Andy and Chris who were off to Bristol to begin the last unit of their course, and then began packing our luggage. The pre-booked taxi arrived to take us to Yeovil Junction train station. The trip to Waterloo Station was quite uneventful, (it must have been because I slept for a good portion of it). **Then we were in London,** *where nothing is uneventful. There was a porter waiting with a ramp. After I was on the platform, he carried our baggage into lifts, doors marked, "Staff Only", until we reached a taxi ramp. London cabs are relatively small but with a, "mind your head guvna" the driver pushed me into the cab via the side door and without ramps. Liz climbed in, the luggage was stowed in the front and we set off to Liverpool Station. Here I posted a reward, "Anyone who knows the whereabouts of the wheelchair-accessible toilet on any of the three above-ground floors, please contact me on this number. Full confidentiality is assured, even for staff members (in the unlikely event that they would be able to assist)". What happened after I found this toilet doesn't need to be described. Suffice to say that the catheter equipment didn't do what it was supposed to.*

At last Liz was relieved of all the baggage by a friendly official who led us to the train bound for Romford. From there it was a short taxi ride, (driven by a West Indian disgusted by England's stalling tactics at the end of the Cardiff Test, and who hoped they would be crushed in the Second Test), to the Romford Central Travelodge. We checked in to a large fully-accessible room, and then did a little shopping. On our return, we met up with Wes who had just arrived from Australia. The Red Lion served us cold beers and good meals at better than reasonable prices.

14/7/09

We took the train into Liverpool Street Station after breakfast at a local café (£4 for a full breakfast). From Liverpool St Station we eventually found our bus to Lords. Why Lords? Because someone left our tickets in Australia! The tickets were replaced, at a fee, and then we saw the Australians training. I declined all interviews with the media scrum, and left. A sign that advised it was a 10-15 minute walk to Baker St Station must have been erected for the 2012 Olympics (for which London is well prepared). We decided, since we were running out of time, to take the Open Top Bus (hop on, hop off) tour. I think Liz enjoyed it from the top deck. From the bottom deck where the driver and I were stationed, my imagination, assisted by the commentary, was taken on a tour of the principal sites of London. Then it was time to head home.

It is easy on a Monopoly Board to find your way from Piccadilly Circus to the Strand. In London, about two correct turns and five wrong ones will get you close enough to ask someone who looks local, (any nationality or language in the world), which way to Liverpool St Station. They are all very helpful.

We arrived back in Romford, met up with Wes and had a "cracking feed" at the Red Lion. Another late night after writing some postcards and updating the diary!

15/7/09

Another late start, breakfast at the same café, then Wes went on a test run to Lords. Liz went back to the hotel and I pushed to every bus stop in the vicinity looking for one where the 252 stopped. That bus would take us to an accessible underground station where we could get the tube to the Tower of London. I never found it, (the bus stop), so we departed on the train for Liverpool St Station. We then took a bus to St Paul's Cathedral, got off, then realised that we had insufficient time to take a tour of this magnificent-looking building, so caught another bus to a stop close to the London Eye. The L/E is 254m high, and, as you would expect, can be seen from quite a distance, but after we got off the bus, it became invisible amongst the high-rise buildings. Having eliminated north, east, south and west, we asked a man in a safety jacket who willingly gave us directions. The only problem then was meeting up with Wes for our 2.00pm "flight". Wes's text message said he was there but clearly we weren't in sight of each other. So the hostess kindly changed our flight to 3.00pm, by which time we had found Wes (or he found us). Our personal guide, dragging a sophisticated-looking esky behind him, led us through shortcuts by-passing the queue and into the next capsule. There were just three of us plus the guide and four bottles of champagne. I knew how generous Fiona was in booking and paying for the champagne flight, but that's a lot of champagne! However, another larger group was booked on our flight and hadn't shown up. The guide pointed out significant landmarks as we climbed higher above the Thames. The 45 minutes went too quickly—we needed a pause at the top of the rotation.

After disembarking, we set off for Ross and Lynelle's apartment close by, but not in, Buckingham Palace. I set the GPS. People we walked past wondered where the voice was coming from. We found them and got dressed (me in slippers because of my sores) for our night out— "Chicago", the musical, in West End. We travelled by taxi. When he pulled up he said, "You be right guvner?" It seemed I had to get in the cab by myself, but with help from Ross and Grant, I was in—no anchorage, no seatbelts. Off we went! We all dined close by the theatre. The performance was terrific, worth all the trouble. However, not all the party agreed, especially Betty who became claustrophobic and had to leave half way through.

Afterwards it was back to Liverpool St Station having successfully found the No 11 bus but it was going in the wrong direction. Eventually we got there, but the lift wasn't working, so I flopped down two flights of stairs with assistance from other commuters. We arrived home at about 1.00am. No diary or postcards last night.

16/7/09

The First Day of the Lords Test! The weather was perfect. I didn't have a ticket. I decided not to go into London but to have a lay-day. Liz went sightseeing in London. She took a cruise on the Thames up to (or is it down to) Greenwich, and then did some washing at the Boyles' apartment. I enjoyed a sleep in until 7.30am. By 10.30am I was ready to go down town (Romford) to have breakfast and watch the cricket. At first I was happy that Australia wasn't batting first so that I could see them on Day 2. Then Mitchell Johnson bowled the worst opening spell since "Daffy" in Brisbane 18 years ago. Only Siddle seemed to make any impression but, by lunch, England was 0/120 at a rate in excess of 4 runs per over. It was sheer carnage!! I left the pub, went back to our hotel, and had a cup of tea while I wrote postcards. Then I went downstairs to write and read some emails.

When I returned to the pub, the English batsmen, Strauss (who had just reached his century) and Petersen were just walking off for the tea interval. Looking at the scores convinced me I had done the right thing in missing the middle session. The third session was probably Australia's.

It was interesting watching the cricket in the pub. Some patrons showed no interest, some checked the score from time to time, while about 5 or 6 of us watched throughout. As well as England was doing, most believed that it only improved their chances of a draw. The bookies—Ladbrokes and Bet Fred—were offering 3-1 England.

When Wes arrived back to the hotel, he and I went out to get something to eat. At 8.45pm only one pub was still serving food. We put in our orders then sat at the only table available. Then a band arrived, set up beside us, tuned up their equipment and, just as our meals arrived, they began to play—very loudly. The lead guitarist was about two metres away. The saxophonist cooled my meal very quickly. As they played, people swarmed around, some presumably attracted by the band. It puts a lot of pressure on two diners whose manners were put under such scrutiny. We ate enough of our meals to satisfy our hunger and promptly left. My ears were still ringing when we arrived back in our hotel. Liz had arrived shortly before.

17/7/09

Liz and I set off early for Lords. We arrived without too much trouble, but, unlike Cardiff, no-one was prepared to show us to our seats/positions until we were in the near vicinity. The officials were mostly service personnel from all arms of the forces from both Australia and the UK. I'm not sure if this was for additional security or the normal practice. It was impossible to move anywhere without showing our passes. When Grant rang me, I was politely told that phones were not permitted in the ground during play.

It was awesome to be at Lords, the "home of cricket", for an Ashes Test despite how poorly Australia played. However, the area they had set aside for wheelchair-bound spectators was at the very back of a grandstand which offered a view of the ground but not much else. I could not see much of the famous pavilion, nor could I see the media centre. A very cold wind blew through the area so that we needed scarves, beanies and heavy coats. I felt we were treated like second class spectators here. What a contrast to the pleasant experience at Cardiff!!

*I expected everything to be quite officious here. I did not expect to see the hostility displayed by the crowd. Being biased is one thing but to jeer Ricky Ponting onto the ground and **then to jeer him off after he was out** was something the like of which I had never seen in Australia. Mitchell Johnson was heckled constantly whether he was on the field or in the dressing room. "Su-per, super Mitch; su-per, super Mitch; su-per, super Mitch; Super Mitchell Johnson" (sung at various tempos for long periods of time). It affected Johnson to the point where he walked backwards to his position at fine leg. I have experienced the "balmy army" in Australia where their singing adds atmosphere to the day's play. But in England they are an ugly group, not there to enjoy the cricket, but to do everything possible to enable England to win.*

We saw the Queen being introduced to the players and officials with the pomp and ceremony associated with such traditions. We could also see Ritchie Benaud ring the bell that traditionally warns players of the impending start to the day's play.

You are probably wondering why I have written little of the cricket. Australia was simply terrible. Two of our key players, Mitchell Johnson and Michael Hussey, let us down very badly.

18/7/09

We left Romford for Liverpool St Station; me headed for Lords and Liz sightseeing around London. We caught the No 11 bus to Aldwich. Liz got out before there. I continued, watching the signs above me indicating the next stop. After a while I asked another passenger when we would be at Aldwich. She told me we had passed Aldwich and that I should get out at the next stop. I got out and so did she, as it turned out, to help me back to the bus stop I needed to catch the No 13 bus to Lords. It soon arrived and she got on as well telling the driver where I was going. Sometimes there's a fine line between feeling patronised and appreciating assistance! What a wonderful person. She told me she was just going shopping and jokingly I replied that I may have at least saved her some money. I began to relax, (which is unwise in London on public transport), when a voice from up front came out with, "Does anyone know where we are?" **It was the bus driver!** *The same lady came to his rescue, guiding him through a number of turns until he found his bearings. In his defence, the normal route was blocked to enable a bike race to occur. It was a Sunday.*

I eventually got to Lords, although at a different gate to the one at which Grant was waiting. Eventually we met up. Then for the tricky bit! Grant had a ticket for me in his stand which I could not access. We were going to bluff our way to the wheelchair area. When the official asked for our tickets, we looked the other way pretending that we knew exactly where our seats/spaces were. The wheelchair area was not full, so I stayed.

The cricket did not improve on yesterday. Still they jeered Ponting, especially when he dropped a catch. Officials fuelled the hostilities by replaying the dropped catch about five times. At other times, there were no replays even of significant events.

The day was even colder. When we decided to leave early at 6.00pm, it began to rain. It is very difficult to get in and out of Lords with few gates and narrow paths. They simply can't cope with large crowds. It may well be "the home of cricket" but it rates well below any other ground I have visited.

As I waited for my No13 bus, the rain got heavier. An umbrella doesn't do much for me! Grant and Betty's bus came and went. After quite some time, the bus arrived and took me to Aldwich. I knew I had to catch a No 11 or 23 bus to Liverpool St Station from the other side of the road. But the other side of the road was boarded up with scaffolding everywhere. It didn't have a footpath let alone a bus stop. I chose to go down the street looking for the bus stop. Eventually I arrived in Trafalgar Square looking at Nelson's Column. So I went back and took a turn in the opposite direction. Bus stops but not the right ones! I continued in a variety of directions until I was again looking at Nelson's Column. Other Australian visitors would have taken photos but I wasn't in a photographing mood. After I had viewed Nelson's Column from all directions, I decided to continue in what I thought was the right direction without turning. Not only did I ask for help, I knew all the shopkeepers by their first name. They were sympathetic but unable to help.

This took me to Piccadilly Circus. Anyone who thinks it's a circus hasn't pushed around it in a wheelchair. Returning to the Square, I pushed on to the Strand. Then a rare flash of common sense told me that by this time, buses to Liverpool St Station would have a different number. So I started to check the maps at each bus stop. At last I found one. I hailed it down; the hydraulic ramp began to come out but then receded. The bus was about to leave. I was pushing the wheelchair button and other passengers were shouting to the driver to stop. So he got out and helped me in through the front door to the wheelchair space. I was so relieved! I told him I was going to Liverpool St Station. He looked at me and said, "You're on the wrong side of the road, we've come from Liverpool St Station"! I wasn't going anywhere. He probably saw the look on my face and suggested I stay on this bus to the end of its run and then wait for it to return to Liverpool St Station. I was more than happy with that, after all, I had just pushed my wheelchair through two cities.

I arrived back at Romford, wheeling past all the pubs which had turned into nightclubs. I entered one, to the surprise of the security guard at the door. I needed a drink! It was just as well I was thirsty because I couldn't tolerate the noise much longer. So I asked for a bottle of wine (which hotels rarely sell, apparently). There was one on display so I bought it (at a very agreeable price) and left. It was 11.00pm when I arrived back in our hotel room.

There must have been some positives:

- *I saw a lot of London*
- *I got a lot of exercise so that I probably shed a kilo or two*
- *I got to meet a lot of people in unusual circumstances*
- *I was much more familiar with Lord Nelson*
- *I had more ammunition with which to criticise that overrated cricket ground.*

19/7/09

The easy thing would have been to stay at a hotel in the centre of London and to travel by taxi. However, it would have denied us the experiences and you, the interest in this diary. To experience a trip such as this involves getting lost and experiencing unusual and unplanned events. At the time they elicit swear words; later they seem amusing; and certainly they will forever more be talking points.

Today I met Grant and Al at Lords without much difficulty. All I wanted to see, knowing Australia had little chance of saving and no chance of winning the Test, was Australia to show some fight. This they did, of sorts, when Clarke and Haddin compiled a substantial partnership, with Clarke reaching his century in fading light. Unlike Grant, I couldn't be tempted to attend Day 5 to see if we could get the 210 runs required with 5 wickets in hand. Anyway, Liz and I were booked on a train to Paris.

We are staying tonight in a hotel in Kings Cross, adjacent to the St Pancreas International Station from which we would leave in the morning. The hotel is quite ordinary but it will serve its purpose.

20/7/09

Gai Paris—c'est magnifique (mostly)! Arising at 3.30am, we prepared for the short walk/push to the Station. We checked in, were assisted on via a ramp and positioned in a special place on the Eurostar. The train left at 5.25am (London time). The scenery in England was interesting, while in France, it was agricultural and eye-catching (perhaps it was the feeling of being in an exotic country—La France, Continental Europe)!

It was only a short time before we entered the "Chunnel". The Eurostar is a fast train travelling at about 170 km/h, with the facilities of an international aeroplane. A sumptuous breakfast was served so that we didn't need lunch. We arrived in Paris at 9.10am (local time—1 hour ahead of UK time). First customs then the mandatory "find the toilet challenge", made interesting by gendarmes patrolling with sub-machine guns. I wasn't game to ask them for assistance. Others offered assistance in a variety of languages, none English. At last I found one and HAD TO PAY TO USE IT!! I wasn't frugal with the paper handtowel.

We found a taxi which took us to the Arc De Triomph, an interesting place of great historical significance to the French. It is located, as Fiona warned us, in the centre of a crazy roundabout where one takes one's chances to get across about 5 lanes and no pedestrian crossings to the Arc. Once there, a very heavy chain fence with narrow entrances (for people not in wheelchairs) surrounds the site. Eventually, some kind and strong tourists helped me in by lifting the chain. We then took a lift to the first floor. Liz climbed the steps to the third floor.

To get a taxi to the Eiffel Tower, we asked an official who just pointed at a couple of gendarmes. They shrugged their shoulders but we persisted. After much waving and gesticulating, (the French tend to do this a lot—even the taxi drivers although I would rather their hands were on the steering wheel), one was enticed to stop.

We arrived at the Eiffel Tower—what a place!! It is so imposing on the landscape that it reminded me of Uluru. The huge crowds formed long queues. In my well-practiced procedure, I asked an official if I could access places in a wheelchair. Mai oui!! He took Liz to the ticket office, made sure we got a healthy concession, and then ushered us past the queues to the next lift. Merci beaucoup!! (You wouldn't believe I failed French at school.) The lift elevated us rapidly to the first floor restaurant and then the second floor observation deck. The view of Paris from here was spectacular, although we didn't always know at what we were looking.

We left the Tower and pushed along the banks of the Seine. Often we stopped to turn around to see this incredible sight. What must it have seemed to people when it was first built so long ago as the then tallest structure in the world?

It was quite hot that day in Paris (27°C) so we soon tired of pushing! We crossed one of the many bridges to find ourselves in a very exclusive shopping area. People were fashionably dressed, filling coffee shops, and filing past shop entrances with concierges. It was interesting just watching them (since we couldn't afford to buy anything).

It was time to get a taxi back to the Gare du Nord. We received the same high class service on our return trip on the train—a complementary drink followed by a delicious dinner. We were soon back in London where we caught a bus to Liverpool St Station and then on to Romford. When the train arrived in Romford, the ramp wasn't ready. Liz got off, the doors closed and I set off for the next station. An official was waiting there with a ramp and a stream of apologies. He got me on the next return train to Romford where I received more apologies. I pushed back to the hotel. Liz was already there. Midnight—an 18½ hour day to Paris and back! But what a wonderful experience!

21/7/09

Since there was no compelling reason to get up early, and since we went to bed very late, we slept in until 7.30am. With some regrets, because we had a wonderful time while in Romford, we checked out. We had breakfast at our usual, caught the train after farewells to the station master who we had got to know well, and departed Romford. This time, however, we got out at Stratford and transferred to the Jubilee Underground line, my first experience of the "tube". We travelled directly to Waterloo Station. There we got on the South West train to Yeovil Junction, where we were met by Andy in heavy rain. However, Andy and Liz loaded up the car and we drove to East Chinnok, our home away from home. The apples had grown, (as had all the vegetables), so that they were showing colour and no longer dropping on the ground. How good it was to have a delicious home-cooked dinner and a fairly early night.

22/7/09

Another sleep-in for me, bathroom and toilet routine while Liz collected our washing from the laundrette! Crepes with myrtle syrup for breakfast, and then we started packing—me supervising and Liz actually doing all the work. The plan was to pack a suitcase with all the things, including presents and books that Liz had bought, that we no longer needed and send it home by ship. The rest would all go in the remaining suitcase so that nothing remained at Andy's and Chris' house.

Andy kindly drove us up to Bath where we met Grant and Betty at a Park and Ride. Later, the Boyles (Ross, Lynelle, Jessica and Penny) arrived on a bus. We packed everything in, somehow, and set off for Monmouth. This was the start of our bus trip and our mutual sightseeing. Much banter began which made the trip a little quicker.

We stopped at the Hereford Cider factory. Liz and I went in while the others went shopping.

Following winding and narrow roads, we arrived at our B & B, thanks to the GPS. We met our genial hosts. They had prepared everything very well for the 8 of us including a booking at the local pub for tea. (Throughout all the UK and Ireland, the locations of B & B's included the distances to the nearest town and the nearest pub. The pub was nearly always closer.)

23/7/09

Staying overnight for 2 nights saved a lot of pain in packing and repacking, as well as giving us an extra night in an excellent B & B. We set off for the Royal Welsh Agricultural Show much later than we planned—this may well become a feature of our bus trip. It had rained the previous day as it does frequently here, so the parking and all the show stalls were mud. I managed to keep much of the mud off my wheels by rubbing them against my jeans. It was interesting to see how different the locals are. Not too many young teenagers in Australia would enthuse over first prize in, "Two leeks on a plate". They were proud of their agricultural lifestyle, and the flowers, fruit and vegetable displays were outstanding.

The traffic gridlock getting in and out didn't enhance our opinion of the event. It was amusing to all except one of us when Grant bogged the bus. We arrived home and set off immediately for the pub for dinner, and got home reasonably early.

24/7/09

We loaded up the bus again and departed Grosmouth bound for Liverpool. And what would I see there!! Once we left the narrow roads and got on the motorways, the trip progressed nicely. The problem with narrow roads is not just that they reduce speed, but they are lined with hedges, mostly unkempt, so there is little to see, including the road sometimes.

Our only stop, apart from getting petrol, was at Ludlow. Here we looked through the ruins of a castle, then spent some time browsing through the markets and the quaint shops. I bought some fruit for which I was pining. It served one important purpose at least, although I wasn't in an appropriate place when it happened. So while the others left to find a restaurant, I, with much assistance from Liz, put things aright. After a nice dinner, we retired to our rooms. It is already midnight and I have just finishing my diary entry.

25/7/09

A day in Liverpool was always going to be a highlight of the tour, and much of it would be spent in the museum of the "Fab Four". I was not disappointed!! The museum was set up very well on Merseyside, of course. It was comprehensive, including music, film/video footage, memorabilia etc. Most displays were numbered and, with a set of headphones and a keypad, I was able to hear documentary as well.

The others in our party had completed the tour and wanted to move on. Betty came back to look for me. I finished the tour at a slightly faster pace and entered the souvenir shop. I already had a good idea of what I wanted to buy—even the type of poster. I had seen it in Chris Turnbull's room in Adelaide. But it wasn't there. I did however purchase some other posters—one for me and one for Pat Drew.

It was 3.00pm when I emerged. Grant and Ross had gone off to see a submarine (I don't think it was yellow). Jess and Penny went to see a Harry Potter movie. The rest of us went to the other side of the harbour to a building with a Slave Trade museum (during the slave trade, ships left from Merseyside to capture/buy slaves in Africa and sell them in north, central and south America), on the top floor; a Titanic museum on the second floor (the Titanic was partly built here; and on the bottom floor was a maritime museum (which contained a ferry which crossed the Mersey).

I started to push back to the bus stop, bouncing over cobblestones and old broken planks. We had travelled to the Docks on an open-top bus which, although it wasn't accessible, could accommodate me if I was helped up the stairs and transferred into a seat. However, that was not possible for the return journey, so Liz and I made our own way back—and surprise, we got lost! But we were not too late, went out to dinner at an Italian restaurant, and later Ross and I shared a port and a cider liqueur (for comparison) and now I am determined to finish this diary entry. A great day!!

26/7/09

We left Liverpool for Carlisle. We were soon in the Lake District, perhaps the most picturesque part of England. The name describes what it is—a series of lakes set in sparsely populated valleys. Lake Windermere is the principal attraction. Here we boarded a car ferry to Hilltop which is Beatrix Potter country. We visited one of her houses. She was so successful with her books (children's books) that she was able to purchase 15 surrounding properties. She was not a capitalist in doing this, but rather was so taken with the area, that she wanted to preserve it. She did keep all the properties as a working estate, but entrusted the land and buildings to the National Trust.

Continuing on through the Lake District we drove through the Cumbria region to Carlisle. A short push/walk downtown saw us at the Australian Hotel where we could buy Tooheys E/D or Crown Lager in bottles, but went to eat at another pub.

27/7/09

The north of England is prettier than the south (that should wheel over a few toes). The Yorkshire Dales and even the Yorkshire Fens take the attention off the roads, which are not as narrow. Grazing of sheep, cattle, dairy and beef, as well as a variety of crops as far as the eye can see.

*We first spent some time looking for a good vantage point to see Hadrian's Wall. This wall, nowhere near the scale of the Great Wall of China, was built under the rule of the Roman Emperor Hadrian starting in 122AD to keep out the marauding hordes from the north. It worked, apparently! It is mostly in ruins but many sections can be seen with **parts** of the fortresses remaining.*

We travelled on to Whitby. It was at Whitby that Captain James Cook completed his indentures as a mariner. It is a very picturesque port on the north-east coast of England. There is a museum there but we didn't get time to see it. It contains many references to Cook, so the brochure said. The harbour where we had fish and chips (of course) had a replica boat and large crowds of tourists. School holidays have just commenced here. On top of a cliff stand the remains of an abbey. Seeing the ruins of castles, etc can become a little "ho-hum" after a while. But with imagination, and the information provided in brochures, one can see in them imposing structures. I felt that we didn't spend enough time here but that was often the case.

We hurried off to see Castle Howard. This stately home is still that. It is also lived in. This was the case in many places such as this, generally so that the owners could earn tourist patronage to help pay for the upkeep. We were greeted there by volunteer workers from the National Trust, who showed us through sections of the house. The house had been partly destroyed by fire. Apparently the garden, including its rose beds and orchards, was also an attraction but it wasn't accessible to me. In fact, the top floor was inaccessible by wheelchair. It was already after closing time when we departed for York.

28/7/09

Another very early start so we could drive to a Park and Ride where we found a bus to take us into York. We headed straight for York Minster, unparalleled by any other church I have seen. Each section of the church contained centuries of history, priceless stained glass windows, each individually designed, and ornate carvings and etchings. It was a mistake, I soon realised, to join a guided tour. Our guide was loquacious to the extreme especially regarding the history and the detail of each panel in each of the many windows. I fell asleep at one stage before receiving a sharp dig in the ribs. After 2 hours we excused ourselves. Liz wanted to see upstairs but she missed the "on the half-hour tour". I wanted to find a toilet but when I did it was out of order. Nevertheless, everyone must see this place (not the toilet—the Minster).

After an argument with a bus driver who wouldn't let me on the bus because there wasn't enough room even though the wheelchair space was empty, and then she let the next 20 people on, I found myself getting angry. It was probably not worth it since it was the wrong bus anyway. Fortunately we met up with the Boyles and found, with their help, a bus to take us back to the Park and Ride.

All present and accounted for, so we set off for Chatsworth House, a massive estate full of priceless furnishings belonging to the Earl of Derbyshire, (Earl No 10). Unfortunately it was raining, (the sooner they fix up this Global Warming the better), so I couldn't see what was reported to be a spectacular garden on an estate that was still a working property. We were the last to leave (what a surprise I hear you say!). A short drive took us to Nottingham and another Travelodge Hotel. As was the case the previous night at a Premier Inn, what they considered to be an accessible room was far from it. I took some angry pills and confronted the receptionist, accusing her of renting out 4 rooms for us while claiming that one was wheelchair-friendly. Lots of apologies but no satisfaction! We enjoyed a good meal, our last together on the trip.

29/7/09

We drove through constant rain, quite heavy at times. Still we kept up some cheerful conversation. We stopped in downtown Nottingham only to find that they had, at last, realised that Robin Hood was a fictitious character and closed down the museum, much to Grant's disappointment. Later we stopped at the Wedgwood Pottery Factory. This place actually demonstrated the art while the real production has moved to China (where else?). Others had lunch here but I was still recovering from breakfast. Food here is a hazard and the best antidote is to watch the company you keep. Australians—disastrous; Andy and Chris—ideal!!

We crept into Birmingham in driving rain and on congested roads. Even with the GPS, we found it difficult to locate the accommodation of each of us. The Paragon Hotel has probably seen better days but is still a "grand old lady". However it was probably built before showers were considered a part of hotel accommodation, and certainly before people in wheelchairs ventured out. It has a bar populated by quite a few Australians obviously here for the cricket. We struck up a conversation with one opposition supporter, who had come down from somewhere for the cricket. He said he followed the cricket and attended every Test Match he could. When I asked him if he enjoyed Cardiff, he looked at me with astonishment and said, "That's in Wales!" He also said he didn't go to London.

30/7/09

A sleep-in until 7.10am! By the time we had completed our routines, it was time to leave the hotel to push up to the car-hire depot where I had pre-booked a car. Out came an A-Class Mercedes Benz with a sunroof, no less!! (All we had booked was a small to medium economy car.) The GPS was charged up and mounted on the windscreen and we set off looking for the canal network. Birmingham is an old industrial centre and in the heyday of the Industrial Revolution, canal transport was essential. We found it but there was no parking close by. It was close to the city centre. Liz walked back to see it but it didn't seem accessible to me. In the shopping centre, we had much trouble finding a place to download photos. But we did, waited 15 minutes, and then found a post-box to send off postcards that were written long ago (especially one to mum).

It was time to set off for our pre-booked Cadbury Chocolate Factory tour. Now many people will have the misapprehension that I organised this tour because of some predisposition to chocolate! It started with a short tour when we were given a number of samples to begin with, and then, at the end, we were invited to choose the ingredients for a cup of chocolate. Remembering Fiona's advice, I chose capsicum and deep sea tuna—NOT! With this boost of energy, we proceeded to the next building for the main tour. It was comprehensive and full of surprises. Our electric car crashed into the one in front, (neither of us was driving), causing great chaos. We were offered, and politely accepted, more samples of Cadbury's best. This was a very popular tour and some in our party who didn't book, missed out.

We returned to our hotel, met up with our English friend who described the first day's play and, as many Englishmen do, concluded by predicting a comprehensive victory for Australia. In the bar we had dinner and a drink then retired to bed. It looked like a bed, but when I transferred onto it, it seemed as though I had missed the bed and landed on the floor! On the brighter side, I have just found out about possible extra tickets for Headingly. I will ring them in the morning.

31/7/09

I was so looking forward to today. I know Australia has played poorly, but they have always been able to turn things around. At 1/126 at stumps on a considerably shortened first day, there was much to expect from the Australian batsmen. That changed after 2 balls. Statistically, Watson had done well as a shock replacement for Hughes, but to get out on the first ball of the second day to an ordinary ball when he should have been looking to get the team away to a sound start was giving the Englishmen a real boost. Then Hussey, the former Mr Cricket, let a straight ball hit his off stump on the second ball of the day—unforgivable. Generally Australian batsmen surrendered for 263. Strauss batted very well to start England's innings—he is a good bat. I have never rated either Cook or Bopara and I was proven correct. I wouldn't be surprised if Bopara loses his place in the team. Otherwise England, despite the weather, is on target for another win, unless rain saves us. The forecast is for more rain.

The crowd here is savage. They targeted Johnson relentlessly when he batted, (for 1 ball), and especially when he was on the field, bowling or not. It is definitely getting to him.

When bad light stopped play, we realised how difficult it would be to get a taxi. So we walked/pushed using the GPS to navigate our way back to the hotel. We arrived without much difficulty but with much less energy. There was a wedding reception in the hotel so the bar was very busy or inaccessible for some time.

One piece of good news did come my way. I was able to get 2 tickets for Day 2 at Headingly. I now have tickets for Days 2 and 4.

1/8/09

Each day brings a new experience!! I went, optimistically, to the cricket. Liz dropped me off on her way to Stratford-on-Avon. There she took the open-bus ride, hop-on, hop-off, which is a feature of most cities in the UK and Ireland.

I collected a newspaper, the Times, which was given out free of charge at the test matches (one of the features of my Scottish heritage). Sitting under cover because of persistent rain, I began reading the cricket news. The rain stopped, covers came off but still no play. I began on the sudokus and crosswords as the rain began again. The ground announcer informed us, I think in a bid to keep people there eating and drinking, that an early lunch would be taken. By 3.00pm I decided to leave despite light rain. Of all the things I learnt in the Spinal Unit, pushing a wheelchair while holding an umbrella was not one of them. By the time I got out of the ground to hail a taxi, I was getting quite wet. Then an amazing thing happened—not a taxi arriving because that would be more than amazing. There were 2 young men who asked me if I was waiting for someone. When I replied that I was waiting for a taxi, one gave me a poncho (unravelled it and put it on me) while his friend held an umbrella over me. They told me this was not the best place to get a taxi, so one pushed while the other kept his umbrella over me as we moved to a taxi rank outside the main gates. The man with the umbrella was "selling tickets". We would call it scalping in Australia. He said the bad weather had cost him money. He also said that he had been to Australia, selling tickets at the 2000 Olympics. His friend was selling ponchos for £1, with all the patter he had learnt. The crowd was flooding out of the gates so one of my helpers offered to buy or sell tickets for Day 4. Some laughingly offered to sell him today's tickets. I quietly told him that if he bought them cheaply, he could pick up a full refund since it seemed certain there would be no play. It seemed the least I could do to repay him.

After about an hour, a taxi arrived. They helped me in whilst elbowing away others trying to use the cab. When I turned around to thank them, they had disappeared into the crowd—2 very suspicious-looking con-men. It reminded me of the lyrics of W S Gilbert, "When a felon's not engaged in his employment, his employment; when the cutthroat isn't occupied in crime, 'pied in crime; they love to hear the little brook a'gurgling, brook a'gurgling; and listen to the merry village chimes, village chimes". The moral being that miscreants have a soft and humanitarian side as well!

While it would be foolish of me to suggest we should trust everyone, I would recommend we never label people with distrust or otherwise because of any prejudice. As it happened, they were both dark men.

I arrived back at our hotel, collected the key, got into our room and started to dry out using the heater. Liz arrived some time later from a very enjoyable day. We had coffee, cheese and biscuits in our room tonight.

2/8/09

Off to the cricket again! The first sight of the day was a cloudless sky. They generally don't last long here. Threatening weather lasted all day but it didn't rain at all. Play was delayed until 12.00 noon. Edgbaston is apparently noted as a poorly drained ground. In the end I saw 6½ hours play, some of which showed an improvement in Australia's bowling, especially that of Johnson. There was also some good batting by England, notably Flintoff and Prior. The Test looks headed for a draw, although England is a chance.

James Davis and his friend were also there. Grant sat with me in the wheelchair area. Liz picked us up and we dropped Grant off at his hotel. This was to be the last time we saw the Ledgers before they returned to Australia.

We had drinks and meals in the hotel bar. Two Australian couples in there were also attending the Ashes Tests. They were from Western Australia. When we mentioned that we were from the Sunshine Coast, one lady said that she and her husband had visited there when their son played in an inter-state Under 16 cricket carnival in 2008. She was surprised when I told her that I convened the Carnival.

Liz is on the internet while I complete this diary entry.

3/8/09

After a hearty breakfast, we checked out of the hotel, loaded our entire luggage into the A-Class Mercedes (with the Sunroof), and set the GPS for Jilly's place in Durham. We were on the motorway by 10.15am. It was an easy drive from what I remember (I may have dozed off for a few minutes). We arrived at her unit in Caraville, Durham City before the projected time of 2.00pm. There were balloons in the windows and Jill was on the footpath. It was so good to see her again. She hasn't changed at all. With millimetres to spare, I manoeuvred the wheelchair into her unit. After a cup of tea and a lot of talking, we drove into the city centre.

We parked in the school car park and got on a bus headed for Durham Cathedral. What an impressive place!! So many of these cathedrals would have been even more impressive if not for the destruction orders of that tyrant, Henry VIII!! A combination of religious intolerance and a greedy desire to take anything of value resulted in the ransacking of these churches. That included smashing the stained glass windows. In this cathedral, some panels were recovered and included in the new windows. We then walked/pushed to the nearby Durham Castle. The Castle has been turned into a university college. Tours were closed for the day but I would not have had access anyway. Instead of taking the bus, we walked/pushed through downtown Durham to the river, recently in flood. The part of the town we saw was a collection of small shops rather than department stores.

On our way back, we stopped at a restaurant where we dined before going back to Jill's place. We talked until tiredness overtook us, and then went back to our hotel.

4/8/09

Not an early start so we arrived at Jill's place at about 10.00 am. She had organised a hamper and we set off on a tour of the district in our A-Class Mercedes Benz with a Sunroof. First we went to Housteads Heritage Park. It required a 1km trek, too steep and too rocky for me. I wrote some postcards while Liz and Jill visited the excavation of the Roman fortress at Hadrian's Wall. The next stop allowed us to drive right up and over the wall (if only the marauding hordes had realised how easy it was). Dozens of cross-country hikers could be seen following a well-worn path along the wall.

From here we drove to Kirkhale where Capability Brown lived. Who is he, I hear you ask? A famous landscape architect of the 18th Century! Most of the craft shops in the buildings were offering expensive wares.

Our last visit was to Woodhorn, a museum dedicated to the coalminers of Northumberland. This was a very interesting tour, although we didn't complete it, which clearly showed the horrendous conditions under which these miners worked. From age 13, boys were woken at 1.00am for their shift underground. When miners were killed, their families lost their houses and their coal allowance, not to mention their income-earner.

We enjoyed a nice dinner and a long chat with Jill.

5/8/09

A late start, a longish breakfast and it was after midday before we left for Annan—our first foray into Scotland, aye. It was such an enjoyable stay with Jill. How often had I said to her, "I'll see you in Durham someday", and deep down doubted that I would ever go overseas? She has not changed—happy, hospitable and fun to be with.

After a short while we changed countries! On a fine warm day we arrived at the home of Jim and Sheila Cowan, parents of Ian. He came to Queensland to teach. I shared a staffroom with Ian for many years. He is a very good Physical Education teacher. Jim and Sheila had visited Ian on a number of occasions and we had the pleasure of meeting them several times.

We had a cup of tea with a jam tart outside in one of the most colourful gardens I have ever seen. Aye, and the vegetable garden was looking grand too Jim! Nearly every plant and shrub displayed vivid colour. Vegetables were also grown in the hothouse so they were virtually self-sufficient.

That afternoon, we drove down to the Solway Firth. Despite it being an A-Class Mercedes Benz with a Sunroof, Jim was quick to point out to Liz that he got so nervous when a passenger in a car driven by a woman that he could scarcely breathe, and sometimes broke his seatbelt. Liz could hardly drive, turning left instead of right, until we came out on the beach overlooking the Solway. We saw 2 fishermen, George and John Willacy, brothers of Sheila, drive out in a tractor, the tide being out. A very old "right of way" had been granted by James V in 1538 only to residents of Annan to net fish in the Solway Firth. Most residents had grown old, lost interest in fishing or found other things to do so that these 2 brothers were amongst the few who continued to net. There was no catch that day. However, the nets had to be repaired and cleared of debris. George blamed the wet weather and the resultant fresh in the rivers causing the salmon to head upstream to spawn. They could use fixed nets, "haaf nets", and pocket nets to catch mainly salmon, trout and mullet. In fact, it was the subject of a TV documentary that we saw later. The permit was challenged unsuccessfully in the High Court. It is a dangerous way to catch fish with shifting sand and fast-moving water caused by the big tides (in excess of 10m). We also saw another documentary featuring Sheila's cousin who operated a shrimp boat on the Solway. One day, while winding in the shrimp net on a steel cable and placing the boat on autopilot, the boat bottomed out. His leg was caught in the winch and was severed. With amazing strength and self-control, he radioed for help, both for his injuries and for a friend to take control of his boat. There aren't any "nancy boys" here!!

George was a real character! Ian's advice was, "when he introduces himself you can believe him, but after that, be on guard".

Sheila cooked us a delicious meal of salmon and garden-fresh vegetables, the salmon having been caught in the nets the previous day, (although part of it had been eaten by a seal on the other side of the net). The night was warm but we slept well.

6/8/09

Breakfast was a fulfilling meal that Sheila had prepared. After loading up the car, the A-Class Mercedes Benz with a Sunroof, we set off on a tour of the Solway and surrounds with Jim and Sheila navigating. Our first stop was at Powfoot which offered another view of the Solway from the western side of the Annan River. Then we headed north to Dumfries, the provincial capital. This is a picturesque city, especially around the River Nith. There are many bridges, both road and pedestrian, and one took us over to a museum featuring Robbie Burns, a poet, lyricist and forefather of Scotland. This year, 2009, is the 250th anniversary of his birth and has resulted in the, "Call to the Clans", to return to Scotland to participate in the celebrations. Being in a wheelchair, I was unable to see upstairs, but a film had been made, so Jim and I sat in a small cinema downstairs to watch the film featuring the life of Robbie Burns.

Our next stop was for lunch, which Sheila had prepared, including a flask of coffee. Liz and Sheila had a quick look through the cemetery there. Finally we stopped at Kippford where we could walk/wheel a considerable distance along the sea front. In the distance, we could see wind turbines in, or nearby, the mouth of the Solway Firth. They can be seen frequently throughout the UK and Ireland, but I had never seen them in the water before. Along the foreshore someone had used debris and an incredible artistic imagination to create all forms of objects.

That night George and Janette visited. We talked cricket, fishing and then about anything which a bottle of Glenfiddich induced.

7/8/09

Awakening, not too early, for another gourmet breakfast, we talked easily through the meal with no plans to leave early for Leeds. George had insisted last night that I watch the first session of the Fourth Test at his place. Jim wheeled me down, exchanging greetings with people in town, and stopping to show me the garage he used to own. Jim still does MOT's and repair jobs for customers who won't accept that he is retired. Meanwhile Sheila and Liz had gone to an organised morning tea with quite a few other ladies for some charitable purpose.

We returned after an exciting session of cricket (with George and Jim also barracking for Australia), to a special lunch that Sheila had prepared which included Haggis—delicious! We said our farewells and departed for Leeds. What a marvellous time it was—Jim and Sheila are wonderful people!!

We crossed back into England and found our accommodation in Leeds without too much trouble.

8/8/09

We left with plenty of time for the Park and Ride near Headingly Cricket Ground. Thanks to the GPS this was not a problem. Our positions for the second day of the Test were at the fence below the Western Stand, a very good position.

With Australia dominating the match completely, one would expect very little banter from the Barmy Army. I took the opportunity to give a little bit back. Michael Clarke and Marcus North batted very well. It was a pity Clarke didn't get the century he deserved. Clarke using his feet and North using his crease upset the rhythm of the bowlers. However Clarke's dismissal when in the 90's was never going to change the course of the game. I am now convinced North belongs in the team. He began very slowly, obviously realising the importance of giving Clarke the strike and of building a partnership.

To look around this ground and try to imagine what it was like when Bradman walked out to bat and completely dominate the Englishmen here (334 in 1930, 304 on the next tour, 103 on his third tour, and finally 173 not out on his fourth and final tour), provided a feeling of pride. His first score was a world record, including 309 on the first day, the fastest Test double-century, his passing the 1000 run milestone in only his 7[h] match—all at the age of 21! They say he was hero-worshipped by the Yorkshire crowd and invited back after his playing days were over.

9/8/09

We set off, a little late, to drive to Doncaster to meet up with Chris Hadley, his lovely wife Melissa, and their one-year old son, Caden. However, since they were living in a new estate, the GPS couldn't direct us to their door, although we passed quite near a few times. Chris was ready to go to cricket. He was playing a one-dayer. We talked briefly and then set off for Manchester.

The souvenir shop at the Manchester United Football Ground (Old Trafford—so that it backs onto the famous old cricket ground), is more like a supermarket. It was crowded with people, some of whom had shopping bags full of very expensive items. We selected a few things for the boys.

On our way back to watch Chris' cricket match we heard on the radio that Australia had wrapped up the Test (in fewer than 3 days). We had tickets for Day 4!

Chris' team had an easy win—by 9 wickets. I met a few of his team mates and talked cricket over a beer. I suggested one or two of them might like to spend a summer in Queensland, playing cricket for Nambour.

We returned to Chris' place where we had a meal and a long chat. Melissa is a primary school teacher so, needless to say, she was doing a great job as a mother. We arrived back at the hotel after midnight.

10/8/09

Today we had tickets for the fourth day of the Test. The Australian cricketers were probably headed for the golf course, some perhaps with slight hangovers. After a continental breakfast at the hotel, we set off for the Fountains Abbey and Studley Royal! It is a National Trust and World Heritage Site. The weather was overcast but it didn't rain. We walked/pushed past the ruins of the Abbey to the Fountain Mill, where once the monks ground their corn. They also generated electricity using river-driven turbines. Some of the equipment is still operating, although only for the benefit of tourists. We then pushed along a trail above the River Skell to the Water Garden featuring manicured lawns, streams and ponds. At the lake, I needed a toilet stop and afterwards a cup of tea (the two are not necessarily consequential). Then, since it was already late, we decided not to proceed through the deer park. By the time we got back to the car I knew I had more than my daily requirement of exercise.

It is harvest time here for fodder. Tractors pull trailers loaded with bales, some wrapped in black plastic (the bales of hay, that is). They seem to have full use of the main roads to do this, and take as much time as they wish. Many bales were still stacked in the fields, surprising since rain was imminent.

The carvery next door to our hotel again benefited from our patronage tonight. Liz is still treating my heels and I am wearing some very trendy strapless sandals which were probably available in Harrods but I bought them in a discount shop in Romford.

11/8/09

It started out as a good day. After breakfast we set off for Scotland—Glasgow via Ayr. The trip through magnificent countryside featured pastures so lush that cattle and sheep were lying down. The further north we went, the heavier the rain became. On narrow winding roads, I found myself watching the road for an inevitable accident rather than enjoying the pastoral scenery.

We arrived at our pre-booked accommodation well before peak traffic. But the room was completely unsuitable, for which the receptionist sincerely apologised, although it wasn't her fault. She made a number of phone calls and eventually found us alternative accommodation at City Apartments (at a considerably greater tariff). By this time I was wondering if I really, "Belonged to Glasgow, Dear old Glasgow Town; for there's something the matter with Glasgow . . ." Finally we settled down to a room-service meal in a stuffy basement room, but with accessible facilities. This room has A FRIDGE!! There was nothing in it, and we had nothing to put in it, but it was a remarkable thing (so I have remarked upon it).

12/8/09

While yesterday was not a good day, today should be bottled and placed on the shelf beside the Glenfiddich. Leaving Glasgow we drove over the River Clyde and were soon alongside Loch Lomond. A vast expanse of water on one side and the Trossacks, often with sheer faces, on the other side of the road (the Trossacks are a mountain range, not a clan)! Here and there were houses, B & B's, hotels and guest houses located in the most panoramic positions. Soon the camera showed, "Card full". So when we arrived in Oban, the first job was to download another 250 photos to disc. I then enjoyed fish and chips on the foreshore of Oban. The town, an old fishing and holiday village on the west coast, is now a major tourist attraction. Some very old stately hotels still retain the prime positions around the harbour. The ferry to the islands in the Irish Sea arrived while I continued to ignore the pleadings of a nearby seagull. You have to eat your fish and chips quickly here because the breeze off the Atlantic is cool, even in summer.

I found an internet café, checked on why I hadn't received my Oval tickets (via Andy), and composed an email to send home. As it was getting pretty close to gloaming we set off back to Glasgow, making few stops before arriving back at our hotel.

We decided to push uptown looking for a restaurant. We ate expensively and therefore frugally. It's a DEAR old Glasgow town! Back to our basement room for a few postcards and a diary entry to finish off a splendid day!!

13/8/09

Today we drove from Glasgow to Inverness. The scenery was as good as and probably better than anything I have ever seen. The mountains were rugged with occasional water courses. Ben Nevis, the highest mountain in Scotland, had pockets of snow left over from winter that we could see clearly from a chalet restaurant at which we had lunch. Loch Lomond and many other lakes were always beside us as we drove through a valley all the way to Fort William on the Road to the Isles. The only problem was an extended delay caused by a fatal accident on a bridge many kilometres in front of us. By using the detour facility on the GPS, we drove an extra 80 km to arrive on the other side of the bridge where we could see a line-up of cars.

Turning at Fort William, we drove eastwards to Inverness, again through a valley caused by a fault line. The road meandered beside more lochs, including the famous Loch Ness. I have to report no sighting of Nessie, which reaffirms my belief that its legendary existence is used to promote tourism. And it works!! Museums, souvenir shops as well as the usual restaurants are clustered around the lake. Urquhart Castle on the banks of Loch Ness was inviting, but inaccessible to me.

Today's trip was another example of Scotland's outstanding scenery. We had dinner at a golf club beside our hotel and, after working out our schedule for tomorrow and completing my diary, we had a fairly early night.

14/8/09

An easy day in Inverness! It was raining steadily which made it quite cool so that I got to use my large jacket again. We found our way into a market area where we had a more than adequate breakfast. I had a haircut and then found a chemist who sold me some enemas without a script. A good morning's housework!

Inverness is known as the City of the Highlands. From here there are several "whisky tours", but I abstained. It is not far from Nairn which is on the east coast. It has its castle and famous old churches as well.

I went back to the hotel, had a nap, and wrote postcards while Liz got the washing done. Again we dined at the golf course since there was no other restaurant close by.

15/8/09

We drove down towards Edinburgh in our A-Class Mercedes Benz with a Sunroof, hoping to visit the Falkirk Wheel. But the traffic was stopped on the motorway. As the minutes ticked by we decided that we had better take the next exit to Edinburgh. Even this took another 45 minutes. We saw a sign, "Road works in progress—Possible delays until September, 2010."

Once off the motorway, we arrived, without further incident to Cockenzie where Ted Anderson and Dee have a very nice home decorated with South African artefacts as a result of the many years Dee lived there before returning to her birthplace. We were warmly received. Ted was one of my closest friends at school in Gordonvale. He lived on a cane farm which his father managed. It was on the way to Aloomba where I lived. Sometimes we travelled on the school bus; sometimes we rode our bikes to school (for me, about 8 km). In class I nearly always sat beside Ted because he was the intelligent student in the class. We played both tennis and cricket together. All these things and many more were reminisced over in the time we stayed there. I left school to go to University in Townsville while Ted went to University in Rockhampton. When Ted graduated he worked for some time in

Rockhampton, was married and had two children. Then he moved to Brisbane; from there to Switzerland and then to Edinburgh.

They had a three-course meal prepared for us, after which it was time to leave for the Military Tattoo. We were attending the late show at 10.30pm. Being a Saturday, there was a matinee performance earlier. Ted drove and Dee navigated to the closest drop-off point near the Castle so that we had only a short push up the Royal Mile.

The Edinburgh Military Tattoo is spectacular to see on TV. But to be there is to witness something special! It is an extravaganza with an excellently choreographed display of traditional pipes and drums, not only from Scotland, but also from other countries. When accompanied by the bagpipes, they make the body tingle. The clever use of the Castle as a backdrop—it changes colours, has images projected onto it, and features in the finale—is a major highlight of the show.

The Chinese performance was very artistic incorporating much of their traditional culture. Perhaps the Swiss band and the Top Secret Drum Corp were even more entertaining. The Australian Federal Police Band participated. Many of the performances featured music composed by Robbie Burns, including, "Auld Lang Syne". After all the performers had marched out of the courtyard, to the accompaniment of the collective pipes and drums, the Lone Piper played under the spotlight from high up in the Castle.

There were no vacant seats. Our area was underneath but at the front of one of the side stands. Consequently, we were very close to the action. The only things we couldn't see were the flyover and the fireworks at the finish.

Ted and Dee were waiting at the same place from which we disembarked. When we arrived back at their place, they insisted I taste some of their whiskies especially the single malts. The drinks helped the adrenalin subside to the point where we fell into bed at about 3.30am.

16/8/09

Some of today I have already chronicled. After a late breakfast (full Scottish), at midday, we drove into the city. Sharing the knowledge and great passion she has for Edinburgh, Dee took us on a sightseeing tour with Ted driving our A-Class Mercedes Benz with a Sunroof. Most of what we saw was the "old city", now well displayed on my camera, I hope! We stopped at a seafood restaurant right on the Firth of Forth, where we dined on local seafood. The mussels, although not as big as mine, were the best I have tasted.

Before going home, we went to Dockside to see the Royal Britannia, now decommissioned and used as a tourist attraction and function venue.

17/8/09

The offer to stay another night with Ted and Dee was accepted (wisely, as it turned out). Liz and I set off on a drive to Dundee. The first highlight was the crossing of the Firth of Forth via a spectacular bridge (beside the railway bridge built earlier). It is an engineering achievement that also offers great views of Edinburgh.

The next stop was St Andrews. Along the way we saw a lot of rural industry, especially wheat farming. I have always thought of St Andrews as "the home of golf", a venue for the British Open. But it is a large town with a widely-acclaimed university and, of course, a castle. So big was the crowd, that we parked a fair distance from the attractions. At the "Old Course" I saw a foursome tee off. They were accompanied by caddies hired from the nearby Caddy Clubhouse. I think it is obligatory. The St Andrews Golf Clubhouse was quite a distance away, and, in the rain, was out of my reach. The museum we saw was largely a retail outlet (and a very expensive one).

We drove on to Dundee, quite a large city (the third largest in Scotland) with an interesting historical dockside. One of the main features was the ship used by Captain Scott (of Antarctic fame) and a museum dedicated largely to him. His ship, Discovery, in which he made his famous voyage to the Antarctic (being the first to reach as far south as 82°S), was moored outside.

We had a late lunch here, walked/pushed up town for some shopping, and then retraced our steps back to Edinburgh (in our A-Class Mercedes Benz with a Sunroof). Dee arrived home from work soon after we returned. She is a personnel officer for a large company. Ted works from home as a consultant on workplace health and safety. Ted prepared us a sumptuous meal which, along with plenty of conversation saw us through to bedtime.

18/8/09

We returned the car at the railway station and, with plenty of time, boarded the train to London. The trip was very comfortable, quick and provided an extensive view of the varying countryside and towns. We arrived at Kings Cross Station (not long after passing GO). An attendant and a porter were waiting with a ramp. They and the taxi driver we soon hired were very helpful although amazed at the amount of luggage we had. In Dundee we had purchased another suitcase to accommodate the extras we had accumulated during our trip. The taxi let us out at our hotel in Battersea.

19/8/09

We left in different directions. Liz went to Madame Taussaud's Waxworks (which was mostly inaccessible for me), and I took a bus to Wimbledon. In my ignorance, I presumed this would take me to the Wimbledon Tennis Courts. However, this was the end of the route so I had to get out. An elderly couple helped me get the bus I needed and, after 4 stops, I got off.

The tour of Wimbledon I found quite ordinary. I couldn't access some of it and places I would have liked to see, such as the players' dressing rooms and entrance *to the court weren't included in the tour. However, for accessibility reasons, when we were shown the Centre Court, others on the tour sat in the stand, while I was on the court itself (millimetres from the playing surface). The "Graveyard Court", No 2, has been demolished and relocated (because of the superstition?). There are over 50 courts, many with artificial surfaces, all used by members except Courts 1 to 4 and of course, Centre Court. These courts are used only for the Wimbledon Championships. The museum was interesting, but I was running out of time (and energy). It was 29°C in London—quite hot given their unpreparedness for high temperatures.*

I set off to find a bus for Clapham Junction. The attendant said the bus stop was down the street and first left. It was a long way to the "first left" and then a steep push about 200m to the bus stop. I started off with grim determination, "I know I can . . . ," but started losing pace rapidly; "I think I can . . ." Then I saw the No 39 bus arrive. I had 15m to go, but had almost come to a halt. I waved to the bus driver and he gave me a friendly wave back. I wasn't sure whether this meant he was prepared to wait. A considerate gardener emerged and gave me a push to and into the bus. I was a spent force!

Without any further trouble I arrived back at the Junction. I alighted down the ramp on 2 wheels as Brooke taught me at the PA Hospital. When I looked about I wasn't sure just where I was. I think I spend too much time looking down at the pavement for holes, broken glass, etc. But I did see The Slug and Lettuce and wheeled straight in there. It was about 3.30pm but I had a beer and a steak sandwich. Sufficiently invigorated, I left in the right direction, picking up familiar landmarks as I went. But often things don't go to plan, as I had frequently discovered, and I was soon lost. The people I asked for directions knew nothing of the Travelodge Romford. So I got out the GPS and it directed me to the hotel.

I was asleep in a hot hotel room when Liz arrived back from her day out. We went out for a meal then had a reasonably early night. The hotel doesn't have an accessible shower (what a surprise!!), so I will have a sponge bath tomorrow morning before heading off for the first day of the Fifth and deciding Test.

20/8/09

The First Day of the final and deciding Test!! I took a taxi, quite early, and met Will at the Alec Stewart Gates. We found our places without difficulty. Then the bad news!!

England won a critical toss (again) and elected to bat on a very good wicket—dry enough to be a third day wicket. Thankfully many gave their wickets away, none more so than Flintoff. His presence in the team would bolster their confidence after an overwhelming defeat at Headingly but if he bats like this, he won't contribute much to their score.

Will was feeling the effects of the previous night's activities, but still enjoyed the day, the first time he had been to a Test here, although he lives close by. For me, to be at the cricket ground where the first ever Tests were played in 1880 and 1882, and to see its iconic gas holders, was a thrill on its own. There is, not surprisingly, much rivalry between Lords and The Oval. Apparently a notice in the Lords' Pavilion asks all patrons to wear jackets and ties. A notice at the Oval requests all patrons in the pavilion not to remove their shirts. Our seating was behind the bowler at ground level, with the curator and ground staff sitting beside and in front of us.

After we returned to the hotel after cricket, Liz, Will's wife, drove over and we went to a nearby Thai Restaurant for dinner.

21/8/09

When I awoke, I noticed that one of the tyres on my wheelchair was quite flat. We wheeled to a nearby service station and pumped it up. I remember telling Will last night that one of my greatest worries wheeling around the back streets was the broken glass that seemed to litter the pathways.

Then we travelled to the cricket by buses. This was easy and much cheaper than using a taxi. It rained late in the morning session so that players took an early lunch. Surprisingly, the press, and many of the spectators, had Australia in the more favourable position. However, with nearly 300 runs on the board and the wicket already dusting up and taking spin on the first day, I know in whose position I would prefer to be.

After a protracted lunch because of rain, Australia struggled to dismiss the tail before England had posted a very good score.

I had not expected to see Australia bat as badly as they had at Lords and again at Edgbaston, but they did. While there was no doubt that Broad, whose position in the English team was not secure, bowled very well, and Swan bowled a containing spell, Australia should have batted much better. The "golden days" of Mike Hussey's career have certainly ended. He is stuck in his crease, is unsure of where his off stump is, and batting like a player hoping to eke out a few runs to retain his place in the team. In short, I think his days are numbered. Again, Watson surprised with another decent score in his role as make-shift opener. Ponting showed his recent bad habit of shuffling across his crease. Haddin, a poor excuse for a wicketkeeper, is now failing with the bat and should have his position reconsidered.

Liz left at 4.00pm to meet Andy and Chris who had come up from East Chinnok to see us off tomorrow. At the time I knew my tyre was nearly flat but couldn't think of anything to do (leaving was out of the question). I asked the ground staff but they just shrugged their shoulders.

As a result of the rain break, play continued until 7.00pm. Although we had 3 wickets by stumps, Strauss, easily the best bat of the series, was not one of them.

I made my way to the gates with great difficulty because of the flat tyre. Although the bus stop was not far away, I knew I wouldn't make it. I explained my dilemma to an official, telling him that I needed to get a taxi at the gates. He asked me to wait until the crowd left, which they did very slowly. Meanwhile, a taxi he had called for me was also waiting outside. It was a sedan, so I had to explain patiently how to take the chair apart. He took me to the same service station, (very rare commodities in London), we had gone to earlier. It was a very expensive trip.

Meanwhile, I was receiving telephone calls from Andy asking of my whereabouts. We had planned to take Andy and Chris, Will and Liz to dinner that night. They were already at the restaurant. I pumped up the tyre hoping that it had only a slow leak. I eventually arrived at the restaurant where we enjoyed our dinner and the entertainment provided by a soprano who used the diners as props for her operatic numbers. I was "lucky"—chosen twice. Perhaps my day's experiences made me seem like a tragic character in an opera.

I was very tired that night making no diary entry, writing no postcards and ignoring the television.

22/8/09

Our last day! I used the shower chair for the last time—no regrets there!! It was dismantled, packed into its bag and left at reception to be collected on Monday. It had served its purpose but was poorly designed. Then we (Liz mainly) packed up the rest of our belongings into 2 large suitcases and a few small bags which would serve as carry-on luggage on the plane. We left these at reception also while we went down to Clapham Junction to try to get the tyre, whose slow leak was getting faster, fixed.

Outside the railway station, a young man pulled up on his bike, locked it to a bike rack, and was about to catch a train to work. I enquired about the proximity of a bicycle repair shop. Not only did he give us directions, but he also extracted a pump from his back pack and pumped up the tyre. We pushed for miles, constantly being advised that it was just a little further on. When we arrived there he said it was probably just a valve (meaning he didn't have time to repair a probable puncture or replace a tube). So we caught a bus back to the Junction where we met up with Andy and went into a pub for lunch. Chris found us soon afterwards. On our way back to the hotel, we found a mini-cab depot and booked one for later in the afternoon. Their mini-cab is what we in Australia would call a maxi-cab. Work that one out!

It arrived at 4.30pm and, with our entire luggage, we all piled into the cab bound for Heathrow Airport. We boarded the plane (BA) after I got very angry with officials who were supposed to provide us with assistance, but hadn't arrived until I had voiced my complaints about the airline. Passengers had boarded when I arrived at the boarding gate, but I told them I needed to use the toilet before boarding. They apologised, waited and helped me to my seat. Foolishly, I didn't use my cushion. Perhaps with time to think about it, I would have.

We departed for Singapore!!

23/8/09

I am not sure when today officially started, but I know I was in an uncomfortable position when it did. When we got out at Singapore for a 4-hour stopover, my wheelchair was brought to the landing chute for transfer. The tyre was flat and the pump was in cargo since they wouldn't allow us to include it in our take-on bags. Changi is a huge airport with a shopping centre, but nowhere was there a tyre pump. So I started to push along the carpeted floor until the tyre had no air at all so that I was pushing on the rim. We were already nearly a kilometre from the check-in for our flight home. So I decided to wheel back but not before I had purchased some duty-free Glenfiddich.

I used the travelator but when it finished so did I. Consequentially all behind piled over top of me. They all apologised, even though it was my fault. I was righted and continued laboriously onwards. I was exhausted when I arrived back at C17 departure lounge. We boarded a Qantas flight for the final leg of our trip to Brisbane.

24/8/09

This flight seemed much easier. I didn't sleep much but listened to some music and saw the beginnings of some awful movies.

When we touched down in Brisbane and were taxiing back to the terminal, we were able to turn our mobile phones on again. A message came through immediately from Greg, "What day are you returning?" Since Greg was supposed to meet us, this created a scramble to reply only to then get another message, "Just joking".

With my wheelchair still unusable, an attendant pushed me in the aisle chair to the luggage carousel and then to the car. While I transferred into our car, Greg and Liz loaded up the luggage. I was pleased to be back in Queensland, but this Global Warming!! We left London in summer on a warm-hot 28°C and arrived in Brisbane to a winter's day with the temperature reaching 36°C. I planned to stay awake to avoid jetlag, but eventually succumbed to the heat and lied down on the bed in the air-conditioning. After a 3-hour nap, I was ready for dinner, some TV, a toilet and shower, and then bed. I slept soundly until 8.00am the next morning. My first sleep-in for a long time!!

Postscript

On reflection, I enjoyed the holiday immensely. The landscapes were so different; the people were quite different; the lifestyle was different. So I witnessed a lot of people living quite different lives to those of Australians.

The chance to meet up with Andy and Chris (in their own community), Will and Liz, Sheila and Jim, Jill, Ted and Dee, Chris and Melissa (and Caden) was really special. The history (our heritage) was interesting and, at times, fascinating. It is well-preserved by the Brits.

The events like the Edinburgh Military Tattoo, the theatre in West End to see Chicago, the flight on the London Eye, the East Chinnok Annual Barn Dance, the Yeovilton Air Display and the Ashes Test Matches are, and always will be, experiences I won't forget.

The cricket!! We lost the Ashes to the better side. Had we won the First Test, perhaps things would have been different. They prepared all their pitches knowing our spin-bowling strength was down. Some people claimed the omission of Hauritz for the last test was a blunder by the selectors. Yet they forget that we beat the Englishmen in less than 3 days at Headingly and our fast bowlers did the job! And isn't the Oval noted as a fast bowlers' wicket as Michael Holding constantly reminded the commentary box! In the end, the dismal performances of two of our key players, Hussey and Johnson, were the telling factor. I hope Ponting returns for another Ashes Tour. I won't be there but Australia will perform much better.

I have now seen the "slope" at Lords, the gas holders beside the Oval; the ground (Headingly) where Bradman compiled his massive scores; the primitive facilities at Edgbaston; and the first ever test in Wales (at Cardiff).

Did we try to do too much? Probably, since fatigue eventually got the better of me! But, what would we have left out?

AND, how did I manage to do all that in a wheelchair? If you have a disability, don't let it prevent you from attempting an adventure like this. Just do what I did—muddle your way through and trust someone will help when it all seems too much!

Mum stayed on in Fraser Shores after Dad's death. She had friends there even though she was a "home person". She loved the garden and tried valiantly to keep Dad's roses going. Gradually we dug them out. Mum kept up the table tennis and some tennis. Even I played table tennis a few times. Mostly, when I visited Mum, I would stay 3 or 4 days. It was good for me because I could push my chair around the streets of the Village, keeping in the middle of the bitumen roads to avoid the camber thanks to the patience and understanding of the residents. During the day we found much to talk about, while at night we played scrabble, a game we both enjoyed. Sometimes we would play two games before bedtime.

Returning from one of these trips to Hervey Bay, I arrived to find that Greg had been involved in a car accident. A passenger in the back seat, he was being driven back to our house by a friend. The car left the road, hit a tree and rolled down an embankment. Greg had been admitted to the Emergency Department of

Nambour Hospital. X-rays showed that he had fractures to his spine. Thankfully, there was no injury to the spinal cord. This section of the hospital was bustling with activity. The staff tried valiantly to tend to the needs of all the patients. Many patients were lying on beds in corridors; many were constantly calling out for assistance. It was not a pleasant place to be!

However, what concerned me most was that Greg had not been stabilised. Having suffered a spinal cord injury, I knew that it was possible that an unstabilised fracture of the spine could pose a danger to the spinal cord. And I knew what that could do! Although he had been heavily sedated, he was still uncomfortable and restless. I tried to calm him down, distracting his attention away from his injuries with topics of various conversations—anything to stop his movements.

Eventually, a nurse who we knew came on duty. She gave Greg special attention. First, she summoned a specialist to complete the diagnosis of his injuries. Then, with the doctor's approval, a bed was acquired in The Royal Brisbane and Women's Hospital. It was decided that it was best for him to be transported by helicopter. The paramedics strapped him onto a stretcher and off he went to Brisbane.

Eventually Mum sold her house and moved in with Jill and Bob. They built a new house at Cooroy. The house incorporated an area that suited Mum well. They are now much closer to me, so that I can get up to visit on non-tutoring days. Jill loves gardening, something she inherited from Mum. So, with Bob doing the heavy work, all three spend a lot of time in the garden. And it shows! Flowering plants dominate, although they supply themselves with a considerable amount of vegetables. Water features, gnomes and garden furniture of various degrees of antiquity make this part of their property an enjoyable place to have a cup of tea.

When I turned sixty, I remember thinking, if I'm allotted my "three score and ten", then I don't have much time left. The previous weekend was a really enjoyable family celebration. Fiona had her thirtieth birthday shortly before and that, combined with Mothers' Day and my impending sixtieth, gave us much to celebrate. Fiona and Jim flew up from Melbourne while Bronwyn and Brett were up from Sydney. Greg and Bec, John and Jess completed the family get-together. Then all were gone, excepting John who became immersed again in his university studies.

So I was back to my old routine. Getting up at about 8.30 am, spending an hour at my toilet and bathroom routine, having breakfast at about 10.00 am, exercising until about midday and then downstairs to turn on the computer! The internet is, "my little window to the world", as Liz's father would say. My email box contains lots of forwarded emails, sales catalogues and sometimes personal letters. I rarely read the news because I usually read the newspaper in bed each night. But today there was comprehensive coverage of the Federal Budget which was brought down last night. However, now most of the significant aspects are released in the days prior so that there are few surprises after the event. There will be much political grandstanding where members from both sides of parliament use superlatives to describe how good or how bad the budget is. The media will include some independent commentary if we are clever enough to find it. *How I hate the media! Not the ABC but the commercial networks! As far as I can tell, they are not interested in the welfare of the public, just their ratings and profits. I suspect news bulletins are prioritised on the basis of, "Do we have live footage? Is it spectacular footage for which we need to attract viewers' attention by stating, "We must warn you that this contains disturbing images"? Do we have interviews with distraught relatives or neighbours?"*

Students arrive after school for their maths tutoring. Then dinner is consumed followed by some television. I go to bed, read for a time and, with some exertion, manoeuvre my body into a position in which I will sleep partly through the night before negotiating a turn to the other side. Initially, I thought the achievement of these things was improving my independence. But now it is simply repetitive. Is this the routine I wanted? I didn't get out much. I'd stopped playing sport. I kept in touch with some of my friends via email, although that was becoming less frequent.

One enjoyable annual event was the annual general meeting of the Antiquarians Cricket Club of which I am a patron. They always invited me to chair their meeting, and then afterwards, to stay and watch the President's v's Captain's 11. It was a good day out!

How long is a split second? As I fell from the tree, I grabbed for a branch which broke, causing me to land at an angle. The angle was the critical factor causing the fractured spine to pierce my spinal cord. Had I time to think, I would have realised that, since I had ring-barked the tree, the branch would be dead and thus quite brittle. Why didn't I try to just jump feet-first? The worst that could have happened was a broken leg! After all, I had jumped many times before. If only a split second was longer! For that matter, why was I up the tree? For a relatively small amount of money, I could have hired a tree feller. Really, I had no equipment or experience to cut down a tree of that size. If only I had thought clearly about it!

After the accident, I was told by so many people of similar experiences they had, but which caused them little if any serious harm. Those stories did little to cheer me up. But what is an accident? An unplanned event sometimes causing unforseen outcomes! Now I have bladder accidents and bowel accidents. Many times I have fallen out of my wheelchair but the outcomes required only that someone or more than one person has to help me back in.

When my mother-in-law moved in, I had not been consulted. If I had, I would have consented, but warned Liz of the difficulty she faced in looking after two invalids. Initially, Mrs Sinclair was quite independent. However, after a short stay in hospital, she required constant assistance. During the night, she would call out, ring a bell or stamp her walking stick on the floor. This would happen quite often, perhaps every couple of hours. The poor lady was getting quite helpless! She also liked to have the radio on through the night. With her hearing difficulty, this meant the radio could be heard quite clearly throughout the house. I could distinctly hear each hourly news bulletin on nights when I couldn't sleep. Sadly, however, she passed away while I was in hospital. A service was held at our place, attended by the family including me, out of hospital for the day.

I had a pressure sore on my bottom—the size of a tennis ball according to the nurse who visited me at home for another reason. She said I must go to hospital immediately and began to make arrangements. I asked to go back to the Noosa Hospital. Dr Smith and Vicky Trevor, the wonderful wound nurse, began treatment—antibiotics, daily dressings and room service. Each day I received comments from nurses dressing the wound along the lines of, "That's one of the biggest pressure sores I've seen!" or "That's in a bad place!" or, the best one, "That must be very painful!" The next time Dr Smith visited, I asked if he would suggest to the nursing staff some favourable comments might, if not speed up the recovery, make me think that recuperation was occurring.

Eventually I was able to transfer onto a shower chair, then into my wheelchair. I was allowed two sessions in the wheelchair of an hour-and-a-half each day. During one of these sessions each day, I would wheel out of the hospital, down to the end of Goodchap Street, along a pathway beside a nature reserve, past a community centre, up a steep hill, along the Eumundi/Noosa Road then back down Goodchap Street to the hospital. These pushes gave me much pleasure (and exercise) and would use up my allowance plus a little more. Back in bed I read my newspapers, delivered each morning, do the crosswords and sudokus, and nap.

SPOT (the Spinal Outreach Team) were due to visit me prior to my hospitalisation. When they contacted Liz to hear I was in hospital, they insisted on seeing me there. The social worker, Karen, began to organise respite care and the repair of my water lift, (which had broken down in sympathy after I was hospitalised), to be funded by Disabilities Services Queensland. I had only just registered with DSQ, not having previously known of their existence.

The nurse, Jenny, inspected my wound. She seemed less impressed than the nursing staff who dressed it. She suggested she would have treated it differently. She also recommended that I not get into my wheelchair until the wound was completely healed. How was I going to tell Smithy this? He would not take this advice well and I had to tell him. "Where was she four weeks ago?" was his reply. He insisted that I use my wheelchair each day, which I did after the following day.

Carey, the physiotherapist, watched me transfer, an opportunity for plenty of advice. She also checked my posture and the suitability of the chair. After I arrived home she visited again, getting me to trial 25" wheels and a wedge she had fashioned to go under my pressure cushion. She also arranged for me to get a "free wheel", an attachment that converted the chair to a three-wheeler with a large wheel at the front so that I could get over rough terrain a lot more easily. In all, she was extremely helpful. The occupational therapist, Chris, checked on the new pressure mattress I had been provided by a sales representative for use by me in the hospital and then to trial at home with a view to purchasing one. Paul, the occupational therapist at the hospital was of considerable help also in this process. By this time, I was familiar with the procedure. A therapist recommended a product which I then had to trial at home. Then the therapist would make an application for funding, generally through MASS who might pay for all or part of it depending on its necessity. I had the free wheel before Christmas and had trips down the driveway and along the road, a surprise to many motorists.

Vicki checked on the progress of the sore from time to time. Eventually, she gave me a date for discharge—when the sore no longer needed dressing. Dr Smith agreed. His report to my GP ended with a suggestion that I had become "institutionalised". I could imagine the smile on his face as he wrote it. He couldn't resist a parting shot!

Christmas 2011! What a wonderful time it was! Fiona, Bronwyn and Brett, Greg and Bec, John and Jess all spent most of a week up here. We spent Christmas Day with Mum, Jill and Bob as well as Jill's family, Tara, Lindsay and Jak.

At first there is the excitement of a family reunion. I realise that such events aren't going to last forever. It will become very difficult to co-ordinate everyone. Then, after they departed, there was a period of time with no tutoring. Apart from some vegetable gardening, my life seemed to be going nowhere. Perhaps my depression was accentuated by the onset of another sore on my foot (in the same place as one which I had fifteen months ago). The doctor's first comment was that I may need to go back into hospital. In the past two years, I have been admitted to hospital four times. Each time it was to treat a wound, the last a pressure sore on my bottom that required more than a month's stay—forty days and forty nights. My wounds heal so slowly and then the area remains susceptible for quite some time. Then, to top it all off, I spilled some hot tea on my foot so that a large blister appeared when my stocking was removed.

I had several trips to the doctor/nurse at the Yandina Surgery. Then Spiritus took over the dressings, visiting every second day, and then twice each week until eventually I was given a clean bill of health (at least for my foot). Spiritus also offered respite care twice each week but I soon declined that service. I preferred to work by myself preparing for my tutorials or tapping away on this keyboard.

An article appeared in a newspaper relating the story of an Egyptian man who, as a result of an accident, sustained a spinal cord injury. He checked into a Chinese hospital for treatment that he had heard about. According to the article, he fully recovered to the extent that he walked out of the hospital. *It doesn't require much to catch the attention of someone with a spinal cord injury.* So I enquired by contacting the hospital. I received information and a short questionnaire from the person in charge. She responded to my questionnaire to say that I qualified. She also detailed the procedures and costs. While I agonised over this, the monthly magazine from the Spinal Injuries Association arrived. In it was an article warning of the unsubstantiated claims of various treatments.

In April, 2012, we flew to Melbourne for six days with Fiona and Jim. We had not seen their new house since its infancy. What an impressive place it is, both architecturally and practically! However, since it wasn't complete (for wheelchair access), we stayed in a nearby motel.

Fiona had made the booking, emphasising that it had to accommodate a guest completely wheelchair-dependant, needing things like a roll-in, roll-out shower. The room was terrible! A high step to get inside, a bathroom too small to manoeuvre around in a wheelchair, a shower with a 20cm lip (far too high to cross in my shower chair), and a toilet I couldn't enter since the doorway was so narrow (and, if I could, the shower chair would not position over the toilet bowl). We weren't able to find alternative accommodation for that or the next two nights. The manager was very uncooperative, claiming he had many wheelchair-bound guests who stayed in that room. He would not come to the room so that I could show him the problems. When he said he knew what it was like to be in a wheelchair, I exploded! Fortunately, the vast majority of people are not like that. But sometimes it takes only one! So we cancelled the payment and tendered evidence to the bank including many photos.

When we returned home, I contacted the Spinal Injuries Association in order to get their support should the incident escalate. I provided them with details and a number of relevant photos. They were very supportive. In the end, the non-payment seemed to be accepted by the motel manager. Another victory for persistence!

Fiona had obtained tickets for the four of us for the AFL game between Collingwood and Hawthorn at the MCG. *Me at the "G"!!* It was a thrill just being there, one of the most famous sporting venues in the world. For me, however, it would be the ideal place to watch cricket. The game was very entertaining with a huge crowd of over sixty thousand in attendance. I enjoyed the spectacle. Everyone seemed to wear items of clothing depicting the team they supported. And they supported vociferously! Yet many Melburnians have probably never experienced a State of Origin match. When Queensland plays New South Wales in rugby league, the game is an instant sell-out, especially when played in Queensland. The game is played in a truly passionate atmosphere which exceeds what I experienced that night. Or was I being parochial?

But the night wasn't over! We joined the crowd headed for the nearby railway station. Two stops later we were in Prahran where Jim and Fiona have a unit and where we had parked the car. On the way we walked up Chappell Street. It was busy with cafes, restaurants and nightclubs from which people spilled out onto the footpath. Melbourne is a different place (or perhaps I'm just a country boy).

For a long time, I didn't use the *free wheel*. Then, when I became concerned about my increasing weight, I decided to try it. At first, I went down the driveway, the easy part since it is quite steeply downhill. Then I started to push back up. Not only was the steepness a problem, but the loose gravel of the driveway forced me to have to lift the front castors of the wheelchair over difficult sections. I needed seven rests to get back up to the house. After a fortnight of this, although I admit it didn't happen every day, I decided to extend the push. My determination was to increase the journey after every seven days of the same distance. Although it was very taxing, I enjoyed it, and the beer tasted better afterwards.

Greg and I travelled to Brisbane by train to see the deciding third game of the State of Origin Series, 2012. Many people criticise public transport in Brisbane, but travelling to Suncorp Stadium and home by train is easy, comfortable and, most importantly for me, wheelchair accessible. We arrived more than two hours before the match was due to start. So we pushed up to the Caxton Hotel. From the time the first such match was played in 1980, this hotel has had a close association with the game. Hundreds of people congregated at the pub before and after the game. From the early days of State of Origin, the two team buses drove past the hotel, one cheered on by the locals, the other appropriately booed. Only recently have authorities deemed it unsafe or unwise—bureaucracy gone mad!

The place was so congested, we returned after only one drink to find our seats in the stadium. Those unfamiliar with rugby league's State of Origin concept should imagine a protracted tribal war in which the States' populations urge on their warriors to fight to the death (hopefully of the opposition). In the lead up to the series, matches are talked and written about to the exclusion of nearly everything else, including the weather.

First we had the pleasure of seeing the Queensland Residents' team defeat the New South Wales Residents. We didn't know the players but we recognised the difference between those in maroon and those in blue. The maroons won—the night's first victory. The main game is preceded by much razzmatazz! The two teams then sing the national anthem, normally used to unite Australians in a contest against another nation, and then they proceed to inflict great damage on each other. The crowd, predominantly Queensland of course, participate in the game with calls of "Queenslander" and boos for the Blues.

At the end of a pulsating match, throughout which Greg and I needed to quench our thirst as the result of the exertion, (fortunately, there is an extended half-time so that we could get to the toilets), Queensland won by one point, thus retaining the title for the seventh successive year. I think that if Queensland prevailed for twenty more years, the crowds, the passion generated by the public in each of the two States and the media coverage would not be diminished. Without much participation in the celebrations, we headed for the railway station to ensure we caught the last train back to Nambour. I was in bed well after midnight, but wasn't tired, the adrenalin still pumping through my body. And all this can be experienced in a wheelchair!

Living the Dream

It just happened! My toes moved, as I had directed them to! Then, like waiting for a long computer download, things started gradually to change. I knew I could probably move my legs because some of the muscles were twitching. But the pain!! Then the joy!

I began the long process of learning to walk again. I had not done so for eleven years. I began resistance exercise when pain was the principal sign of progress. My goal now was to walk, no matter what it took. The years of stretching and passive exercising of my legs, as well as the severe spasms that plagued me, were paying off. I had retained some muscle definition.

Initially, I was still very dependent on my wheelchair. But now, I could stand, with assistance, to sit on the toilet or on a chair in the shower. These small things had given me tremendous possibilities. I could access almost any shower or toilet. It was some time however, before I ceased catheterizing since it was the only way to completely empty my bladder. Likewise, I continued to use enemas. Eventually these became too painful and I had to rely on my special diet, including drinking a lot of water, to successfully move my bowels. But although the goal looked distant, I continued to progress. Like a child waiting for a birthday to come, I was seldom satisfied with the speed of progress. I knew it would be exponential, but around each corner was a longer road. I decided to keep a record of my recovery. It became a ledger again, but this time I was reducing my disabilities while my abilities increased steadily.

First I progressed to walking, unassisted (except for the "wheelie walker"), around the house. The next challenge was to do it around the yard on uneven ground. There were falls, but they became less frequent.

It all began to unfold so rapidly. I could walk along the road, up and down stairs including into the public pool where I no longer needed my vest to swim. Each visit to the pool resulted in more lengths being swum.

Then came the start of the cricket season. Perhaps I could fill in—play for Fourth Division. Why not commit for the whole season? But I would need to be able to run. So I tried, and fell over! The opposition, however, was quite obliging, allowing me a "runner" when I batted. I resumed my customary position in slips while we were in the field. Painful, frustrating, but enjoyable! My only success was being able to play.

So why not tennis? I began to hit a tennis ball against a wall. I had to be careful not to swing too hard since that sometimes caused me to overbalance. It seemed no time at all before I was back playing veteran's tennis again. My ability had diminished significantly but my determination partly compensated for that.

Then the Antiquarians began their season and I was on the bus for a weekend away, playing cricket against one of our traditional rivals . . . .

Lindsay, Lindsay, the phone is for you!

Afterword

Now that I have finished the book, I feel a profound sense of achievement. I set out to chronicle events of my life that would be of interest to my family, particularly my children, and close friends. I also felt the need to do something which, had I not experienced the life-changing event, would not have otherwise happened.

After reading and re-reading the book, I am convinced that I achieved more. This book will inspire someone, hopefully many people, with a serious disability to strive to achieve more; not despite their disability, but because of their disability. I also expect that those people who have helped and supported me (those mentioned in the book and many others as well) will realise the fruits of their endeavours, some of which are recorded in this book.

Yet, accepting all these things, I am still thoroughly convinced that I am just an ordinary bloke.

Lightning Source UK Ltd.
Milton Keynes UK
UKOW04f2245281013

219966UK00003B/691/P

9 781477 153215